The Journey of
REDISCOVERING
Me

THE JOURNEY OF
REDISCOVERING
Me

UNLOCK YOUR VOICE AND
REWRITE YOUR STORY

SHERINDA PRINGLE

CITI OF
BOOKS

CITIOFBOOKS, INC.
3736 Eubank NE Suite A1
Albuquerque, NM 87111-3579
www.citiofbooks.com
Hotline: 1 (877) 389-2759
Fax: 1 (505) 930-7244

Ordering Information:

Quantity sales. Special discounts are available on quantity purchases by corporations, associations, and others. For details, contact the publisher at the address above.

Printed in the United States of America.

ISBN-13:   Softcover   979-8-89391-931-8
                   eBook9   979-8-89391-935-6

5 Star Review
Hope resilience and faith!
Stephen Anderson

I love it from start to finish. I love this could be a movie. It was so many different factors that me and my family have went through so many similarities and it was so empowering and I was very engaged in the book and it taught me how to evolve into something great and speak life over any situation And just hold onto God's unchanging hand This book is very aspiring to everybody, especially visually impaired people and people with disabilities and it's so powerful as far as walking by faith and not by sight and just being resilient and hopeful for everything this was such a great read

5 Star Review
A book that connect to all people.
Anthony Villa

Pringle invites readers to release worldly boundaries and open their minds to endless possibilities. By sharing her own story, she persuasively argues that we can achieve our hopes, dreams, and aspirations simply by believing.

5 Star Review

Get This Book

Amazon Customer

This book!!! This book!! This book!! I finished it in a day and a half! Oh my God...it blessed my soul!! I found myself not being able to put it down!! I laughed. I cried. I reflected. Then I got empowered. Empowered to revive my hopes, faith and dreams and to reclaim my life! This book is a must read!

5 Star Review

Woman of God on her journey

Sherise Frazier

Interesting story!! The strength she had to open up and share her story, wow!! A wonderful insight on how this women of God over comes her grief and sorrows. The you!!

5 Star Review

A book that has reflections to human experiences.

Armida Wagstaffe

Sherinda Pringle's The Journey of Rediscovering Me is a deeply personal and inspiring memoir that chronicles the author's path through life's challenges, guided by an unwavering faith. Pringle offers readers a glimpse into her world, reflecting on tumultuous circumstances and revealing the profound lessons learned from each struggle.

5 Star Review

Its unique story to read and makes me connect with it.

Jenna Lee Dy

The book's tone is consistently inspiring and candid, reflecting Pringle's deep personal connection to her story. It explores universal themes of resilience, spiritual awakening, and the power of faith in overcoming adversity

5 Star Review

Highly recommend

Katherine Anderson

Sherinda refused to confine herself. Raised with strong family values, she faced pain and unpredictability. Her admiration and expirations lead you to ponder back in time. Her poetry is genuinely exceptional.

5 Star Review

You Just Never Know

Littlewillie34

I was looking for something to read and found this book. The narrative story caught me off guard. I didn't see the "main theme", coming. Pringle shares a personal story that allowed me to stand right next to her, feeling the path she has walked. I highly recommend this book. I listened on audible. The narrator was great letting me feel all of Pringle's emotions. One other thing, she also sheds light on the emotional roller coaster her husband may have felt which is often left to reader's imaginations. Good work, Pringle.

5 Star Review
A Phenomenal Testimony of Faith and a Must Read
Robin

I was gifted this book during one of the worst times in my life (the passing of my beloved mother) . This book helped me to refocus my grief . This book is a true testament of faith that is relatable to many of life's challenges . This book answers questions we are sometimes too afraid to ask ! If your soul needs a hug buy this book ! The story will speak to your soul and bless your heart !!!

5 Star Review
10/10
Khemra Anetera

I highly recommend this book. It was very empowering and eye-opening. A lot of great sentiments to take away.

CONTENTS

Foreword

This is not just a book—it is a call to journey. A journey of rediscovery. A journey of believing beyond what you see, even when the path feels uncertain. Rooted in the promises of Psalm 91. These pages remind you that though trials, obstacles, fowlers, and snares will come, you are covered. As you walk through the fire of uncertainty, distractions may surround you, but faith will carry you forward.

This is a story of FOCUS. A story of Facing fear, Overcoming trauma, Converting mindset, Understanding the molding in the journey, and Strategizing through boundaries. Each step is an act of courage, each moment a testimony that God's protection is greater than the challenges before you.

Here, you are invited to trust Him fully—to believe beyond the visible, to embrace the unseen, and to claim the promises that await. This is your rediscovery. This is your voice. This is your story reclaimed.

Chapter 1

STRENGTH IN THE MIST

How the hell did I get here? This is the question I asked myself as I lay my big, funky ass in the bed. I had been in this bed for almost seven months. My only relief from this room was Thursday—a standing appointment that I looked forward to as much as I dreaded. I lay here, thinking about the many crazy things that had happened in my life to this point. This raggedy room was actually an accomplishment. I will never forget the day we purchased this place. How could I? It was a supposed three-bedroom apartment in up-and-coming Woodlawn. Supposed, because the third bedroom was so small my big ass would have felt suffocated in it, in my state. The stackable washer and dryer were tucked neatly in the closet. There was just enough room for a desk, a computer, a chair, and some filing baskets. My goals and dreams, my aspirations, now lay tightly tucked away in that room.

We purchased this condo during such crazy times. I remember rushing to get my eight-year-old son ready for school, trying to find my shoe so I could make it downtown for a meeting, and my husband yelling, "Hurry up! We're going to be late." *Good Morning America* was on in the living room. I always watched the news in the morning to stay informed about the world and to make sure my area was clear to travel. Chicago is a beautiful city, but you better keep your head on a swivel and watch your six. Boom! I ran to the TV with one shoe on. This must be a new movie preview. It looked so real. I was half paying attention. My son and husband had just left. I'd better be ready to go downtown when my husband came back. Boom! I heard it again. "A second plane has flown into the Twin Towers." What the hell? I sat and I watched. Unfortunately, it was not a movie. I did make it downtown that day. Afraid to lose the job I'd just started. Downtown was chaotic. The roads were crowded; the subway was shut down. Downtown Chicago was officially a no-fly zone, and it appeared as if the world would never be the same. The next day, we were at the title company, ready to sign on this condo. Almost everybody we knew had advised us against it. "We're going to war," they said.

My husband and I had already been to war. Two naive kids raised on the South Side of Chicago in the heart of the *crack* epidemic. Shit, we were going to closing. Couldn't nobody tell us anything.

There were so many wonderful times in this condo. Of course, we did go to war. The way we traveled changed forever, and the world was completely on guard for years to follow. We, the citizens of the United States of America, also continued to live life. We refused to be held captive, and many brave citizens had already proven that, though we are a dysfunctional family, we will risk our lives to protect our own. In the meantime, this place was always filled with music and people. I have the largest family. On holidays, I would easily have sixty to seventy people in this place. We could laugh, drink, and get full on the food that my family and I prepared. I'm not going to say that there was never a disagreement, but we never fought. We partied, had fun, and lived to party another day.

All those people were in my house at one time and now I lay here alone waiting, waiting for my son to come home from school and waiting for my husband to come home from work, waiting to see what was going to happen at my next Thursday appointment. Thursday was the only day I had to get outside and socialize. I get an opportunity to chat it up with the other expecting mothers in the lobby while we munch on apples and granola bars decoratively placed in a bowl in the center of the coffee tables. It seemed like it took forever for the nurse to call us to the back. I didn't mind though. I was outside. I had an opportunity to feel free of the walls that confined me in that condo. I felt like I was in solitary in the joint. Nobody came to visit me anymore. Sixty people were in my house for the holidays, now I couldn't even get a phone call. It's cool though. At least I have Thursdays.

Faith

They say time heals all wounds; I pray that is true. I have been terribly wounded and in a hurt state of being for a long time. Things are about to change for the better—a new beginning for sure. We have lived in this condo for four years. We have met some really good friends and, as usual, a few of the neighbors are a little complex. The couple across the hall are strikingly peculiar. They have two of the most beautiful dogs, an English mastiff and an English bulldog.

The couple on the third floor, artists from New York, gave birth to the most amazing woman—their daughter. She came to Chicago to stay with them shortly after 9/11. She told the story of walking with her daughter to school when the crash happened; the sound, the smoke, and the smell of human flesh burning had traumatized both of them. She and her daughter came to Chicago to find a new beginning. She needed a job, and my employer needed a surveyor to assist us at the office. I happened to be on the interview team. Many people interviewed for the position. She was the perfect fit. She became my colleague as well as one of my dearest friends.

I had been an active member of the condo association for all four years that we have resided in this vintage six-unit brownstone building. The six-unit Greystone, vintage building adjacent to the south of us made up a twelve-unit association—a wonderful mix of sorts. I was currently the building manager, a job that I completed quite proficiently from my bed. Everyone around me was so nervous. The constant walking on eggshells as though the bottom was literally going to fall out was driving me crazy. I get it; we've all been here before. They were afraid of another heartbreak. Were they protecting themselves, or were they protecting me?

I can't go without mentioning the amazing couple in the next building. Ms. Irvin made the best chicken this side of Kentucky. We loved having board meetings at their home. It was the food for me. They were also one of the sweetest, most generous couples I had ever met, and prominent in their own way. They hosted the Obamas on several occasions when he was making a run for the Illinois Senate. We all have regrets. One of my biggest regrets is not accepting an invitation to have lunch with the Obamas at the Irvins' place. I missed out on breaking bread with the couple who would eventually occupy the White House because we needed to go grocery shopping. Priorities, huh, or lack of. At any rate, we spent a lot of time in the Irvins' home arguing over the assessments generated by the old boiler system in the basement of our old brownstone. It literally gets hot as hell in here. I spend an enormous amount of time working with the management company's maintenance staff to keep the bill down. We spend a ridiculous amount of time bickering over an enormously expensive bill that we have no control over. One of the many reasons that we have decided to buy a single-family home.

I also had the pleasure of working with the groundskeeper. He was so fine. Every time he asked if I needed the hedges trimmed, I blushed. He was caramel-colored and chiseled, a Puerto Rican masterpiece. Watching him and his crew cut the grass was a healthy way to let time go by. My husband jokingly referred to him as my baby daddy. The thought never crossed my mind, but if cheating is ever on my to-do list, um, I digress.

Managing these buildings planted a seed in my head that is dormant for the moment. My dream is to own a courtyard building or ten, with at least eighteen units in each building. Somehow we started out working with a real estate agent to look for buildings and we ended up looking for ridiculously gigantic homes. The first one I saw was so beautiful, the Egyptian Museum. I had just come home from church when my husband ran into the house, short of breath, and yelled, "You have to see this."

When I entered the building, the real estate agent smiled. "Here she is. He almost fell down the stairs to get you. He was so excited." It was a four-level Greystone corner unit that was literally a renovated museum. It was absolutely beautiful. We ran through the home like children, in awe of the vintage sculpted architecture mixed with modern flair. Having been deemed a historical landmark, the stained-glass windows were still intact.

I remember showing the home to my husband's grandparents. They had come to the home to pray with us. My grandfather-in-law wasn't very spiritual. He did acknowledge the universe as he got older, noting an entity greater than himself. His wife was a different story, a God-fearing woman whose prayers made the earth move. "Do you want this house?" she said.

We responded, "Yes."

"Point to it and claim it. Claim the house of your dreams."

We pointed to the house, and we prayed for the house of our dreams. There were several difficulties that transpired after we put the contract on the house. After countless phone calls, arguing with the attorney, and several meetings with the owners, we stopped fighting for the house. My husband and my son were so disappointed. My husband had been forced into church his whole life. My spirituality is far greater than the number of services that I have attended. I have been through many hardships and struggles in my life.

I believe just what grandma said, "You can have whatever you say." My husband's faith is a little wavering. As long as things are going well, he has faith. As soon as assurance dwindles in what he is able to see, his faith diminishes. This time he shocked me. We were driving around one weekend, a few months after we lost the Museum, as I like to call it. He stopped the car and jumped out. "This is it," he said. It was a vacant lot with a sign. The sign had a picture of the most elaborate limestone home. It was four stories, including the basement, loaded with five bedrooms, four bathrooms, a wine room, a theater room, a sauna, a dock, two balconies, and a three-car garage with a deck on top. I honestly thought he had lost his whole mind. He was quite serious. He immediately dialed the number on the sign and scheduled an appointment to meet with the developer.

I can honestly say that though some people consider me to be *bougie*, I am a humble and simple person. My initial thought was, *This house is too much.* Don't get me wrong; I like nice things, but this was a bit over the top. I had so many fears and worries about this one. The elders always say, "If you're going to worry, don't pray, and if you're going to pray…," so I went along with it. I have a way of convincing most people of leaning in the direction of my idea. Somehow this persuasion never worked on my husband. I remember back in the day when we were dating, my cousin came to visit from Dallas. She was young and fine. I guess it runs in the family. We hooked my cousin up with my now brother-in-law and went out to dinner and a movie. It was such a beautiful summer evening in Chicago. The streets were packed with people looking to have a good time. Hyde Park was full of life, and so were we. We were so young and carefree. We thought we knew everything. We didn't have a clue.

It was a little past midnight, and businesses were starting to close. We stopped by the liquor store to grab a pack of wine coolers, gently spiked Kool-Aid. We didn't really drink, and it was all we could afford. Everybody was headed to the beach, and we needed to secure our spot while the getting was good. We were on the strip on Fifty-Third, about two blocks from the beach. This was the shortest route to the beach. It sure as hell wasn't the safest. Lakeshore Drive, an expressway with stoplights every mile, separated us from the beach. I wanted to walk to the light on Fifty-Seventh Street to cross safely.

My husband agreed until his brother and my cousin started clowning him. I was seemingly adamant about walking to the traffic light; I was literally on the verge of a panic attack. All of a sudden, I was alone. I pleaded with them to the point that they were in agreement. I guess the he was still feeling punked by his brother. Out of nowhere, he pointed out that we were wasting too much time. He started walking toward Lakeshore Drive, and all of us, including me, followed. I continued to voice my fear. They clowned me while telling me it would be okay. In a flash, I started to second-guess myself. *Maybe I am too cautious and uptight*—the things they were saying as we reached the drive and were preparing to cross.

They could see the cars slowing down as the traffic light was changing going north. "Run!"

I started to run, then stopped on the yellow line as though I was jaywalking on a residential street. I turned my eyes south and focused in on the lights of the many cars that were about to come my way as the light was about to change. They had made it across the street. I stood by myself in the middle of Lakeshore Drive.

"Run! The light is about to change. Run!" they yelled.

Somehow, I unlocked my feet and ran for my life, landing my body to safety just as the cars began to take off, speeding down the drive. He apologized as he cried. We all cried and took a second to acknowledge God. They went on to continue the evening as though nothing had happened. I assured them that I was okay. I was not okay. I was, however, grateful that God is omnipresent amid my stupidity. Now I find myself again, a deer caught in headlights and praying for the best.

We sat through that scheduled meeting and several more over the last few months. I looked over so many paint swatches and materials. I had the opportunity to design the home literally from the ground up, and I enjoyed it. Now we're waiting. Over the last several months, I had the opportunity to put a contract on the home, assist with its design, and get pregnant. Now I lie here in this bed and wait. I had faith that this house and baby would be brought into the world successfully.

Birthing a book

Yes, today was Thursday. I had an opportunity to go outside. Every Thursday, I got up and took an extra-long shower, and combed my hair, kind of like I was preparing for a date. This date was special. I was going to see my high-risk obstetrician. I had the pleasure of receiving services from the head of the department. He made me a promise twenty-two weeks ago, and I held him to it. His promise did come with stipulations, though. I was not to leave my home until Thursday. I had many opportunities to rip and run the streets, but I declined every offer presented to me. No shopping, no hanging out, no dancing, etc. The most conflicting stipulation was also obeyed. I had not made love to my husband in twenty-two weeks.

Unfortunately, he did not seem to understand our current dilemma, though the doctor had explained it to him. He had become pretty good at leaving me alone, but that's a story for another day.

At that time, I was goal-oriented and wholeheartedly engaged in a successful ending by any means necessary. When I returned from the doctor, I completed my ritual. I got something simple to eat. I had been having difficulty holding down food lately, but the doctor wasn't concerned, so I wasn't either. After eating my granola and yogurt, I cleaned myself up, put on pajamas, and got back in my bed. I spent a lot of time alone. My son stayed at his aunt's house to hang out with his cousins, and my husband was a truck driver, so I didn't see him that often. If I were naive, I would believe that he had picked up more hours at work and hung out with his friends more to deal with the many things that were stressing him out. At any rate, he always brought home a meal for us to eat.

Every so often, a relative dropped by for a few minutes. It seemed as though it was impossible to get people to stay longer than an hour. It was cool, though. Actually, it really wasn't, but I was trying to convince myself that it was. I had been debating the idea that loneliness and being alone are different situations.

I enjoyed the opportunity to meditate and reflect on life occurrences when I was alone. Sometimes I sat in bed and cried. I knew that I was a conqueror. Born to a single mother in the projects, Mom did the best that she could with what she had. We had some hard times. We never embraced the idea of being poor. I was born visually impaired. I'm not blind. I don't see well either. To a blind man, I see everything. To a sighted man, I see nothing. I'm not sure if my family ever even noticed that I was different. "Stop it." I must laugh at myself. Folks in the Black community are quick to ignore things that we don't want to address. Of course, they noticed. To date, it has not been a topic of conversation, not even with my husband. I managed to earn my master's degree and become more employable. Getting through school was challenging. It takes a certain type of deception to act *normal* when you know you're not so others are more comfortable.

I never paid attention to how frequently the home phone rings when no one is home. The phone had rung five times in the last hour, mostly telemarketing calls. Earlier today, the phone rang. On the other end was a pedophile. When I answered the phone, he asked if my mother was home. At first, I laughed. People always tell me that I sound like a kid. For the sake of my own entertainment, I said, "No, my mom is at work," as if I could actually get out of bed to work a job, I thought.

This creep went on to ask, "Where do you live? So I can come play with you." I quickly turned into a full-grown woman on him. People who prey on children should have a very uncomfortable place in the pits of hell. After calling CPD nonemergency to report the creep, I went to sleep.

Just as I began to doze off, the phone rang. It was Girly Girl. I met her about six years ago. I had just finished my undergraduate degree in criminal justice. Given my circumstances, I should have been elated. I should have felt more accomplished, but somehow, I didn't. I was still missing something. Incomplete on life's journey, I was led to an agency that assists people with rebuilding their lives. My correlation with this agency was ambiguous. Destiny's enlightenment would prevail later.

I was so excited to hear from Girly Girl. She always had an enlightening word. We spoke for a while about my current situation. After having the welcome outlet to vent, Girly Girl offered, "You should write a book."

"About what?" I replied. Who in hell would be interested in my messed-up life? I was still so young, confused, hurt, and bitter at the time.

Sixteen years later, after healing my fractured mind and heart, I realize that my journey is an intriguing and necessary story. Perhaps brief darkened moments are meant to enlighten others.

Chapter 2

FAMILY VALUES

Imagine the ability to travel through time. If you could travel into the future and get just a glimpse of your life. I often pondered the idea. Would it be beneficial to jump back into the past to repair some of those jacked-up blemishes, or are those iniquities, trials, and tribulations actually intentional? Every experience in life has value, especially the ones that cause initial shame and embarrassment. Our mistakes become our successes, and our downfalls become uplifting. One of my favorite sayings used to be, "To be young again, shoot me." I grew up in a traditional Black family that had migrated from the South. My mother was always around, but my grandparents raised me. My grandparents raised all of their grandchildren with Southern values. Whether that was good or bad is still yet to be decided.

Mama was born in 1924, and Daddy was born in 1918. By the time I was twenty years old, they had been married for fifty years. Momma was the epitome of a down-home housewife. I can vividly smell the scent of homemade biscuits and fried salt pork with Alaga syrup. At the break of dawn, every member of the household had no choice but to awaken to the aromatic fragrance of fresh breakfast. The modest four-bedroom house was always filled with relatives, and there was always enough food available for those who wanted to eat. Mama was always my biggest role model. Women from that era poured all the love they had to give into their families. Strong as a lion, their shoulders held up their husband and stood in the gap to raise their children's children when needed.

Daddy grew up as a sharecropper. As a young man, he became one of the first men to learn to work the heavy field machinery. He was forced into the field because of his skill and never learned to read. He and Mama left Mississippi when my mother was three years old. They traveled around the Midwest until they made their home in Chicago. He landed a job at R. R. Donnelley, the publishing company known for printing phone books back in the day. He worked long, hard hours in the cafeteria of the publishing company to provide for his son and seven daughters. They started in a one-bedroom apartment then moved to a larger apartment in Chicago's public housing, and finally were able to purchase a single-family home. Daddy prided himself on never accepting relief or public assistance of any kind. His motto was the biblical scripture, "A man who doesn't work, doesn't eat."

Every few months, his job would gift him the most beautiful leather-bound books with gold-trimmed pages: *Moby Dick, Gone with the Wind, To Kill a Mockingbird*—the list goes on and on with the literary classics that had been bestowed upon him. The books were never properly displayed for us to enjoy them. Daddy would bring them home, unbox them, and place them neatly on the closet shelf. As a young girl, I would get his permission to pull the books from the shelves so that my cousins, my older sister, and I could play school with them. Eventually, we learned to read them.

The many things I learned from Daddy. Above all, he taught me how to be loved by a man. He was hard as hell on his daughters, but his granddaughters were a refreshing opportunity for a do-over. He was highly critical of the men in our lives. The many blunt questions he asked us: "Why doesn't he ever pick you up for a morning date? If you work for minimum wages, and he works for minimum wages, why do you need him? If y'all are splitting the bills, can't you get a roommate, and you won't owe them anything?" The old wisdom that most of us ignored hits a little different now. Daddy felt like a man was supposed to be a provider, *period*. The mixture of Mama and Daddy's old-school wisdom molded me.

I had many conversations with my grandparents and my mother. Somehow, we never got around to in-depth discussions about relationships—I mean the love between a man and a woman, sex. All I knew for sure was that sex led to pregnancy, and that if I got pregnant before I finished school, my mother and grandparents would shame me to death. Mama and most of her daughters were mothers at a young age. Of course, this was normal during Mama's era. She married young and gave birth to nine children. Children were encouraged due to a need for hands to work in the field. Unfortunately, this was stereotypical behavior for Black women in my mother and aunts' era. Crazy how the women were shamed and belittled as though they had impregnated themselves. At any rate, the evolution of the woman had occurred in my family. My sister and I had managed to finish high school without getting pregnant, the first to do so in years. Though my family members thought this was a gift-worthy accomplishment, there was zero complexity. My sister and I had high school years that were so tumultuous that we had no interest in dating or sex.

I remember being twenty-two years old, in community college, trying to figure out life. I had worked for Spiegel, a mail-order catalog company, for three years prior. The company started laying off and eventually went out of business. After being laid off, I enrolled in school. I had very little experience with men. I had had a boyfriend but wouldn't consider it a relationship. During the time I worked at Spiegel, I got my hair done every week at a shop on the corner from where my aunt lived. When I finished my appointment, I would always stop to visit with her and my little cousins. I was such an insecure child in a woman's body. I hid it well with the dominating walk given to me at creation—the ultimate deception. Seemingly beautiful in the eyes of many. Financially, nobody could tell me anything. It was 1990. I was living with my grandparents and making three times the minimum wage. I've always liked nice things and bought what I liked. A woman being able to take care of herself was an anomaly. People who didn't know me thought I was being kept by a dope man. After all, it was the '90s. My aunt and her old man lived in an apartment above the restaurant where they worked. The door to the apartment area entry was always locked, leading me to have to enter the store to use the payphone to call upstairs. One day as I entered the restaurant, I caught the eye of one of the cooks, and he was bold enough to speak to me. Most men thought I was unapproachable by the way I carried myself. Honestly, I liked it better that way. All I knew about men at that point was that Daddy was right: Men would tell you what they thought you needed to hear to get their needs met. Being natural hunters, they are more than willing to put the work into bagging what they thought was unobtainable.

He saw something he thought he wanted, and I had no intention of giving it to him. I did, however, entertain his efforts. I offered him flirty and facetious responses, but he wouldn't let up. The more I played with him, alluding that he had an icicle's chance in hell, the more he put pressure on my relatives to convince me to go on a date with him. One thing led to another after my aunt and uncle convinced me to go out with him. The story gets long and complicated, so I'll table it for another day. Its relevance to the current topic is that I ended up pregnant. I had just gotten laid off from my job, I had just finished my freshman year, and I was pregnant. I was unmarried and disappointed in myself for the poor decisions that I had made. I was a statistic, another link in the generational chains that shackled the women in my family and my race. How would I explain this to my grandparents, the only ones who believed in me? I felt as though most of my other relatives had no expectation that I would finish school. They expected that, though prolonged, my destiny would lead me to be another unwed mother. Their thoughts were not malicious. It just was. Hell, very few women from where I come from escape single parenthood. I told my then-boyfriend about my circumstances.

By the time I got pregnant, he was no longer working at the restaurant. He had just started driving trucks over the road and exploring the country. I had started my sophomore year and still didn't have a clue. As I look back on the situation, he wasn't even my boyfriend. As most women did back then, I made the assumption that he was my boyfriend. We had spent a lot of time together over the last few years but had never established a title for our relationship. Now I was pregnant, and we saw each other once every six weeks or so when he returned from over the road. This was cool though. Absence makes the heart grow fonder, or so they say.

Admittedly, we both had mixed feelings. Life was so uncertain then, and neither of us wanted to be parents.

Many thoughts went through my head. The one that continuously lingered scared me, even though it seemed to be the most realistic solution. One morning, haunted by the thought that would not escape my mind, I jumped on the CTA bus and headed west. I ended up at a clinic that I had passed quite frequently over the years while going thrift store shopping with Mama every Monday and Wednesday. She referred to it as *shaking rags*. It was her hobby of sorts. She didn't have a lot of money but still loved to shop. It was her favorite pastime. She had the gift of finding the most beautiful garments. When she finished washing and starching those rags, they looked brand new. After she added her accessories, baby, you couldn't tell her she hadn't stepped out of *Ebony Magazine*.

I got off the bus and walked into the poorly painted building. If it were not for the signs that clearly identified the building as a place of business, it would look abandoned. I walked up the rickety stairs and sat down to wait for my turn to be triaged. I thought about the many times I had placed judgment on women who had previously climbed the same raggedy stairs to the second floor of this *bando* and found themselves in the hot seat.

After what felt like at least an hour, a woman came out of an office with a clipboard. "Complete the forms," she said. The questions on the forms were intrusive, to say the least. Never mind, I couldn't breathe. I answered the questions about my most intimate sexual habits—things that we were taught never to discuss. Just maybe if I had had the discussion with someone close to me, I wouldn't find my dumb ass in this dilapidated building. I handed the woman the clipboard with the completed documents attached and was told to go into the third room on the left. My hands were shaking so badly that I nearly lost my balance as I went to sit. *You're here now*, I thought. *Time to put your big girl panties on.*

I was surprised by the layout when I focused on the room I had entered. There was a comfortable chair and a stool for the doctor, normal for a doctor's office. Tucked in the corner was a television and VCR setup. Needless to say, movie time was not on my agenda when I entered this building. After a few minutes, the doctor came in. She positioned the chair, which reclined into an examination table. After confirming what she already knew from the urine test I had been given earlier, she reviewed the questions and the responses I had provided. She then explained that I would have to watch a movie before she could proceed any further.

After pushing play on the VCR, she left the room. I was nervous and confused as the movie started. I will spare the details of the graphics of the movie, as well as the overwhelming emotion as I took in dreadful scenes that I can never forget. What I will say is that a woman's right to choose is important. Most women in this position take the decision very seriously. Everyone who had walked up these stairs before me had their own reasons and their own limitations. No one has the right to judge. If a woman made that choice after going through the process of watching an act that I cannot describe without tears, it is her choice to endure that pain. It is most likely one of the hardest decisions that she will ever make, and if she has a soul, it will greet her nightly for the rest of her life.

Some will say that there is a level of deception on behalf of the clinics that provide this service. I can say that I am eternally grateful to have been deceived and to have had an opportunity to rethink my initial decision. I couldn't—and I didn't have it in me.

Chapter 3

THE GIFT

I went to church with my family as I did every Sunday, but this Sunday was special—it was Mother's Day. We spent the afternoon at Mama and Daddy's house after church. We laughed, ate, and reminisced about the joyous, funny, and even sad events that had occurred as we looked back over our lives. There is nothing like the sweet moments in that house. I sat patiently in the living room waiting for my mother to give me a ride home. The crowd had died down, and the house was almost empty. Mama looked at me and smiled with an absolute look on her face. "You're going to have that baby before day in the morning," she said. I had been to the bathroom to pee about five times within the last three hours. I was still not concerned about labor or delivery. I didn't have a clear understanding of the prophetic abilities of the elders at that time. As a matter of fact, I strongly disagreed with her.

It was the end of the term, my sophomore year. I had final exams in the morning. The baby was not due for two weeks. This baby would have to wait to grace the world with its presence. Again, she smiled, not bending from her previous statement.

The overwhelming shame and disappointment I felt as I attempted to hide this pregnancy from my family had somehow turned into an overwhelming level of love and support, especially as I approached delivery. I had denied this pregnancy until it became apparent. I had become so huge when I was about five months' gestation. As I toddled to the bus stop one morning, a group of kids yelled out, "Free Willy. Free Willy!"—the title of a popular movie about a whale. I was appalled, but I had to laugh. I could not deny that I was as big as a whale. It seemed like I had blown up overnight. Of course, my family already knew. They had to have known. A family of women, my mom, my little sister, and I tracked the uses of feminine hygiene products. Huh. We'd gotten that down to a science. After all the anxiety and drama, mostly in my head, it was almost time. Two weeks, or at least I hoped.

I attempted to get a full night's sleep. We'd gotten back home from Mama and Daddy's house pretty late, and I really needed sleep to focus on my finals in the morning. I was so uncomfortable. It seemed like I had been to the bathroom at least ten times, and my stomach had been cramping. It was hard for anyone to sleep that night. My mother and sister lay quietly as I wobbled back and forth to the bathroom repeatedly, groaning from the discomfort. At about 6:00 a.m., I went into the bathroom to shower and get ready for school. Regardless of last night's events, I was going to take my final exams.

After managing to get dressed, I attempted to put my shoes on. I had about twenty minutes before the next bus was scheduled, and it was going to take me a while to walk two blocks to the bus stop. As I maneuvered my body to get my shoe on, a sharp pain overtook me, and I fell to the floor. My mother finally opened her door. "Where do you think your stupid ass is going?" she blurted out.

"I'm going to take my finals," I explained.

My mother jokingly told my thirteen-year-old sister to help me put my shoes on so I wouldn't miss the bus. My sister walked toward me just as I yelled out an excruciating groan. She screamed and ran in a panic. When I asked her to come back to help me, she said, "I can't, if I get the smell from that pregnant juice, it will never come off me." My mother and I laughed so hard. That was the dumbest thing

I had ever heard. Mom helped me put my shoes on as she continued to chuckle. I let out another groan as I asked my mother to meet me at the hospital in about five hours, at about 1:00 p.m. I would be done with my finals. My only reference for experiencing childbirth was with my oldest sister. I supported her in the birth of her sons. Each time she was pregnant, it took at least eighteen hours. I figured I could take the bus to school, test, and still have plenty of time to make it to the hospital before it was time to give birth.

I walked out of the front door and attempted to navigate the three flights of stairs required to get out of the building. I got down the first four or five stairs before I belted out a painful groan. At this point, my mother was no longer willing to entertain my foolishness. She grabbed her car keys and asked my sister to help her get me down the stairs. Mom was off work on Mondays. Her weekly routine included going to get gas from the local gas station after she took all of our dirty clothes to the laundromat. They were on the same lot, so it simplified her errands. She had not had an opportunity to get gas, which she noticed when she turned the ignition. My hospital was at least seven miles away from the house, and she didn't feel as though we had enough gas to make it. She sped out of the parking spot and sped to the closest gas station, which was about a mile away. As she pulled into the parking lot of the gas station, a panhandler lay in front of the tank that she was approaching, and he refused to get up unless she gave him money. As my mother attempted to compromise with the man, I informed her that I had to push. Mom put the car in reverse as she yelled at the man, letting him know that he needed to move. The man rolled over just enough for her to reach the tank to pump gas. The station was full of people who were rushing to get gas before they went to work. He was harassing her with the only available pump. She warned the man as she pumped that he had better be gone by the time she finished. She promised him that she would surely run him over if he was still there.

When she finished pumping the gas, she sped off and never looked back. He had been warned to get up, and I was in too much pain to notice. No exaggeration, we were parked at the entrance of the hospital in less than five minutes. There was a nurse entering the hospital as she pulled up. My mom explained to the nurse that I was in labor, ready to push. The nurse went into the lobby of the hospital and returned with a wheelchair. She helped me out of the car and into the wheelchair. She began to assess me as she pushed me into the hospital. I told her that I wasn't scheduled to deliver for two weeks. The baby felt like it was coming. I imagined I had probably been in labor for about six hours. I honestly had no idea how long I had been in labor. I had been uncomfortable since yesterday afternoon at Mama's house.

At any rate, the nurse smirked and directed my mom to park the car and meet us in labor and delivery. She then stated with a lot of sassiness, "These young girls kill me. Coming in here thinking that the baby is just going to fall out." Mom went on to park the car as the nurse pushed me. I felt another sharp pain and explained to the nurse that I was experiencing pressure and needed to push. She blew me off again as she took my vital signs and proceeded to ask me to open my mouth and stick out my tongue. When she stuck the popsicle stick-like contraption down my throat, I started to throw up. I'm thankful that her reflexes were on point. She jumped back before the funky liquid poured from my mouth. I only got the tip of her shoes.

As I humbly apologized, she said, "Maybe you are ready." Then she went to get the doctor. The doctor helped me onto the bed and began to examine me. After examining me, she made an emergency call for the medical team to bring in an IV and get a delivery room available stat. She simultaneously explained to me that the baby had crowned and was only being held in by the amniotic sac. She further explained that she needed to pop the sac so that the baby wouldn't suffocate. As she broke the bag, she begged, "Please do not push." It took a few seconds for the medical team to rush into the room and roll me to delivery.

The whole thing happened so quickly. We had left the house at about 7:30 a.m. Now I had been rolled into delivery, attached to an IV, and commanded to give one strong push. I pushed with all the energy I had left as the doctor guided the baby out of my womb. Delivery time: 8:09

a.m., the doctor noted. I had just been taken to recovery and given a few refreshments when my mom ran onto the labor and delivery floor. She anxiously requested to be taken to her daughter. The greeting nurse smiled and said, "Girl, you can calm down. She's in recovery eating a bowl of cereal. You have a healthy grandson."

"You can't be serious. I was only gone for ten minutes. I just paid $20 for parking, and you're in here eating," she said. I shrugged my shoulders, and we both laughed. We rejoiced in the fastest delivery ever; we were so happy to welcome the healthy new addition to the family.

The birth of my son was so smooth and quick. Many things could have happened. I could have attempted to get on the bus to take finals that morning, risking giving birth in the street or on the filthy bus. I could have pushed after the doctor commanded me not to. The urge was tremendous. Pushing could have resulted in breaking my son's neck. Life is full of "what-ifs" if we choose to think that way. Life is about trusting your instincts and allowing God to order our steps. When we are going off track, he always has a ram in the bush, the reason I gave birth on my mother's day off. I was so hellbent on completing school that I was not thinking clearly. I ended up receiving a final grade of an A in three of the four classes. As life would have it, I had one instructor give me an incomplete and forced me to take the class again. I took the class over and passed. My schedule was delayed by unforeseen circumstances—a small bump on a tumultuous journey.

Chapter 4

MISCARIED

Being an adult in the '90s was magical. The music was amazing—Mariah Carey, Mary J. Blige, Michael Jackson, the list goes on and on. R&B and hip-hop ruled the industry. I loved to sing and dance. I was a twenty-five-year-old mother. I didn't have the opportunity to get out to party often. My son was two years old. My now-husband and I had moved into our first apartment in Hyde Park. While dating, we walked past the building every weekend. I remember the day we were on our way to see a movie at Harper Theater, he looked at the building and said, "I am going to live in this building one day." A few years later, with a child, we were both tired of living in various situations within our moms' homes. At the time, we just wanted to be together. He was finally making a decent salary, and I was in my senior year of college. We went through a management company in Hyde Park, looking for somewhere safe to raise our son. Though I had decent credit and he had a decent salary, the management company did not want to rent to us.

One day, I was going through the newspaper checking for apartments for rent. I came across a one-bedroom apartment with a dining room and a living room. I called the number several times but couldn't manage to get anyone to answer. About two weeks passed when I answered the phone, and it was an older white woman on the phone. "Are you still interested in renting a unit?" she said. At this point, I had made at least fifty phone calls and had no idea which unit she was referring to. She explained that she owned a quaint sixunit building in Hyde Park. She had inherited the building through her husband's family when he passed away. She went on to say that the University of Chicago had been trying to force her to sell for years. She argued she was an old woman, not in search of riches, just wanting to help small families get started in a safe, comfortable place. We chatted for about an hour. At the end of the conversation, she gave me the number to her management company. "Tell them that I said if you want it, it's yours," she said, with a radiant smile that I could feel through the telephone. I still had no idea where the apartment was so I called and made an appointment to see the unit and sign the lease.

We met the man who managed the unit at the office. Ironically, it was the same office that initially denied our application for any unit. The agent who had previously denied our application appeared offended to see us back. It didn't matter; this time we were not there to see him. I smiled at his rejection and politely asked to speak to Mike. He stood as I said his name, and he told the rude dude that Ms. Harris told him to expect us that morning. We did the initial paperwork before seeing the unit. Honestly, it didn't really matter where the unit was or what it looked like. We both needed to move, and the owner of this unit demanded that we stay there regardless of the company's rules. My husband presented his income documents and ID and then went to work. He left it to me to go view the place and make the final decision.

The agent and I walked and chatted as we ventured off to the building. Out of curiosity, I asked Mike what had provoked Ms. Harris to call me to give me the apartment even after the management company had warned her that statistically, we would probably not be able to honor our lease. He took Ms. Harris to be mean, stern, and feeble. I shrugged my shoulders. He continued to talk, confirming Ms. Harris's story, stating that their relationship was better when her husband was alive. He took a deep breath, then he said, "I would sell to the University of Chicago if I were her." We had walked a few blocks, and I admit I was not paying attention to where I was going. "We are here," he said. I focused on the parking lot we had just crossed, the grocery store, and the other convenience stores within the shopping center across the street. It was the exact same building that my husband had pointed at and proclaimed that we would live in. Tears came to my eyes. I knew that my child and I would spend many days alone due to my child's father being on the road as a truck driver. This place was such a blessing. Of course, I was not able to drive. This place would allow me to maintain independence while raising my son.

Mike felt however he felt about Ms. Harris, but I could honestly say that I loved that woman. She followed her heart, understanding the risk. The many gifts she gave me in the process—her heart, her hopes, and her dreams aligned with my own. To have the power to defy rules for the sake of lifting others. Ms. Harris did what she wanted, and she wanted to help me and my family. We had so many good times in that apartment. At that time, family was everything. My sister-in-law had small children like me. We spent many hours in her basement. The children would play as we talked while she worked as a hair stylist. My sister-in-law, my free-spirited hero.

May she rest in peace. Jasmine and Ashley, the two perfectly pedigreed Lhasa apsos that she decided we would share, add to the memory at hand. I'll never forget the day my husband brought her home. The cutest little terror took every opportunity to make a chew toy out of my good shoes. Jasmine made our family whole. As with any young family, we had our ups and downs. Through it all, we grew personally and professionally. We were comfortable with our situation and thus excited to find out that I was pregnant again.

He had been growing in the trucking industry, and I'd finished grad school and landed my first gig related to my field of study. I loved my job. I worked to assist public aid recipients who were blind and visually impaired to find employment. I don't recall feeling stressed. I recalled feelings of joy and accomplishment. Life was good. We moved into a larger apartment, he was on his third car, we had extra money in our budgets for outings every weekend, and we were happy. I was about four months pregnant and carefree. We decided to catch a movie. The newest Batman movie was out. We both loved all the DC movies. We never missed an opening show.

This Saturday, our son spent the night with his cousins. We were eager to catch a movie without the responsibility of a child. After checking to make sure we were not leaving anything behind, I decided I had to use the restroom. A simple task, or so it seemed at the time. He rushed me as usual. It was a crime to miss the movie trailers. I pulled down my pants, sat on the toilet, and felt the need to sneeze. I felt an enormous amount of pressure. Honestly, my first thought was that my bowels were moving. I looked into the toilet and saw blood. Somehow, I rationalized the situation; it couldn't possibly be what I thought it was. I was young and healthy. It couldn't be what I thought it was. I grabbed a few sanitary napkins, placed them in my panties, and cleaned myself up. As I pulled up my pants, I prayed that the blood would stop.

We left the apartment and headed to the movie theater. With foolish faith, we purchased the bucket of popcorn and settled in to watch the screening of our favorite movie. About twenty minutes passed when I felt a huge gush in my pants. I went to the bathroom to check myself. As I attempted to walk, the cramping pain expressed a matter of urgency. Initially, the bleeding had slowed down. It came back with a vengeance. It was not going to stop. I alerted my husband to my issue. When he finally digested what was being told to him, he rushed me to the hospital.

Hospital horror

He was in a controlled panic when he assisted me out of the car and into the hospital building. He alerted the hospital staff member at the front desk that I was four months pregnant and bleeding profusely. The woman looked up and stated, "She probably is having a miscarriage." She proceeded to hand him a clipboard. "Have a seat and complete the documents. Someone will be with you soon." I couldn't believe the lack of empathy as another cloud of blood fell into the third, almost-full sanitary napkin.

I went into the emergency room public bathroom to attempt to clean myself. I checked my purse. I was out of hygiene products. Desperately, I proceeded to stuff my panties with tissue to prevent blood from running through my pants. I had asked the hospital staff for sanitary products, and they said that they were not able to help me. As I think back, obviously, I was worried about the wrong thing. Literally hemorrhaging to death, I was concerned that people would see the blood on my pants. We have been taught to keep ourselves clean at all times; it was considered nasty if someone knew that you were bleeding.

Needless to say, I had no previous frame of reference to deal with or even comprehend what was happening to me. I had been sitting in the emergency room for over an hour, bleeding profusely, and I had not been triaged.

One thing I knew for sure was that my emergency was not a concern of the hospital staff. My husband was angry and noticeably afraid. He walked to the desk again to express the matter of urgency. I sat in pain, attempting to hold back tears. Raised to withhold emotion, I verbalized, "I'm okay." Clearly, I was lying. The next twenty minutes felt like three days. The triage nurse finally acknowledged my name. After receiving my most vital information, my insurance, she began to take my human vital signs. An hour and a half had passed before my situation was acknowledged as critical. I had already miscarried. The afterbirth was not releasing, and my blood was not clotting. I was literally bleeding to death.

The medical professionals immediately prepared a room. The obstetrician on call explained the situation as she rushed me into a room. "If I don't perform a D&C as soon as possible, you will be in jeopardy of losing your life." A member of the medical team directed me to place my feet in the stirrups. The doctor then yelled in disbelief, "Where is the IV?"

She proceeded to grab my hand and rubbed it. "I am so sorry," she said as she held back tears. She let go of my hand and placed it in my husband's. "I don't want to do this, but I must. I have to complete this procedure, and

I don't have time for them to run the IVs. It is going to hurt like hell, but you will survive."

She proceeded to complete the procedure, a D&C with no anesthesia. A D&C, for those of you who do not know, is defined by Google as dilation and curettage, a surgical procedure in which the cervix is dilated so that the uterine lining can be scraped with a spoon-shaped instrument to remove dominant tissue. In short, it felt like my uterine area was being scraped with a razor blade. I dug into my husband's hand for dear life. He braced his hand to endure the pain as he openly expressed his fear. The many things that went through my head: Who would take care of my son? I squeezed, and I endured. Finally, the pain stopped, and it was over.

Chapter 5

FINDING JOY

Please correct me if you believe I am wrong. These are my thoughts as I perceive my Creator and his genius. Everything we do stems from the aphorism of the nineteenth-century German philosopher, Friedrich Nietzsche: "What doesn't kill you will make you stronger." We were born with the innate urge to push through our fears and struggles through our free will, the choice to fight as opposed to quitting—resilience.

Briefly consider one of the elements: water; the same water that quenches our thirst, keeps us clean, and irrigates the land for nourishment will surely kill us if we jump into deep water clueless about how to swim. It's funny how fighting the water will pull you under while relaxing and going with the flow will keep you afloat. If this is true, it would behoove us as a people to relax. Maybe we could survive undesirable situations if we acknowledge that the ultimate finishing move in fighting is to coast the water in our life, gliding and floating until we slide into land.

There is absolutely no way to downplay the utter terror that comes with bearing a child. It is the experience of what we know as a medical phenomenon. Risking death to bring about life, the life cycle would have stopped shortly after Eve if we were not willing to succumb to the pressure of possibly dying in childbirth. Philosophically, the end justifies the means for the continuation of all species delivered through a female. Less profound is the pure joy of human extension of oneself, the thought of loving and raising someone with the potential of carrying on our culture and legacy. My beliefs may be far-fetched to some. I believe that each spirit born into the world has a purpose. The aborting of the body for whatever reason does not negate the fact that the spirit will continue to fight to enter this world for the opportunity to live out its purpose. In my mind, I had no choice but to try again. The strain on the relationship and my lack of emotional stability for some reason had minimal relevance.

Faith

Shortly after the miscarriage, we became pregnant again. The fear of conceiving was expected. I was fertile as a bunny rabbit. Would I be able to carry this baby to term, though? That was the huge question. A few women I worked with were compelled to share their stories of miscarriage with me. One woman shared that she had had her three children after a miscarriage. "It's just something that happens," she said. "It's not a big deal." My doctors were very encouraging. They suggested that we try again as soon as possible. Mission accomplished. We were pregnant. The goal was to stay pregnant. The many testimonies and the overall positivity of everyone around me made my husband and I feel great about our situation. We quickly embraced the new opportunity.

We were initially afraid to broadcast the pregnancy. When people in my outer circle inquired, I ignored the question. I would rather have them believe that I was just picking up weight. I had little tolerance for the gossipers who get some type of sick joy from preying on people's downfalls. At about twenty-five weeks gestation, I began to have more faith that the goal of delivering a healthy baby would be completed. I had been eating healthy, and I decreased my activities. I did continue to work and sing in the choir at my church. I was still in the habit of rushing. Looking back at the new job I had landed after being laid off from the previous one, it was stressful. At the time, I thought it was good stress. You know, that stress that pushes you to bring your A game.

I remember being in the office, rushing to prepare for a presentation. I quickly printed out the PowerPoint slides and rushed to the train station. I was running pretty late for my meeting. This particular day, my immediate supervisor, who usually gives me a ride to presentations, decided that he would drive in from home. He informed me at the last minute. Competition was fierce. It did not pay to be smart, attractive, and a woman. I was still learning the details of a nonprofit social service agency. Some of my colleagues were trying to make it difficult for me. I was okay with that; I appreciated the challenge; I had lots to learn about this agency.

You would never know that I was new to the company from the way that I presented the agency programs to other companies. Somehow, in my shyness, I found my comfort and confidence on the stage. The center of attention in a room full of people is where I found my zone. My whole spirit lights up when I speak about something I'm passionate about. God's ray of sunshine gleams on me now as it did then. I was passionate about providing information, education, and counseling to people with disabilities and limited financial resources.

My destination on this given day was the Mayor's Office for People with Disabilities. They had just been awarded a new grant and the agency needed its best people to go out and sell our services. I ran down Hamlin to catch the blue line train downtown. I was careful to pace myself. After all, I was young and in pretty good shape. I just made it to the top of the stairs as the train was approaching the platform. I was going to be late if I didn't catch this train. I sighed in frustration as the doors began to close, and then like magic, as I got close to the end car, the door opened again. I was shocked when I boarded the car. To my surprise, my sister's baby daddy, the father of my nephews, had seen me running and was gracious enough to open the door, which stopped the train from moving. "Hey, sis!" I hadn't seen him since the twins were babies in the hospital.

My sister has six boys. The twins were a shock to everyone, including my sister. My sister and he had a volatile situationship, to say the least. One night we received the call late in the evening. It was my nephew's father on the phone, very calm. "She is bleeding. Someone needs to come and get her." They had a history of fighting, and we were tired of it. That particular evening, we decided to put an end to it. My mother went into her bedroom and searched the dresser drawers to grab her BB gun, which was a replica that looked like a real .47 Magnum. My youngest sister had a steel baseball bat, and I had a knife. If my sister was bleeding, we were determined that he would be bleeding as well.

We pulled up to the six-unit building in Woodlawn on a mission. We left the car doors open and the car running. We were greeted by the usual group of neighbors who sat on the third-floor stairs and smoked crack while playing music and disturbing the whole building. We approached them, and my mother requested that they move out of the way. One of the women sitting on the stairs responded, "Make me move." My mother pulled the BB gun out of her pocket. She requested again, "Move the ——— out of my way." The group parted like the Red Sea to allow us a path. As we ran up the stairs one of the neighbors yelled frantically, "All you had to do is ask," followed by, "Run, boss, run. They're coming." My oldest nephew opened the door. We ran from the front to the hall in the large vintage apartment, to the back of the hall where the kitchen was located. My nephew's dad had already planned his escape through the back door. By the time we made it to the back door in the kitchen, he had already run and jumped off the second-floor porch, landing like a cat before taking off through the alley. As we reentered the apartment, we could hear my sister letting out a painful yell which changed our focus immediately. We walked into the front of the apartment and entered her bedroom located by the front door. There she lay in a pool of blood. According to the boys, who at that time ranged in age from seven to four, their dad was not responsible this time. They explained that she had gone to use the bathroom and started to bleed as she crawled back into bed. We called an ambulance, then got back in the car and met her at the hospital. We sat in the emergency room for hours with no report. We were finally told that she had been rushed to labor and delivery.

To make a very long story short, she delivered twin boys at twenty-five and a half weeks gestation. The twins had their trials and tribulations, but they survived. My sister finally had an opportunity to escape her situation, and she did. She moved out of that apartment and never returned. Now the twins were about five years old, and I was face to face with their dad. He looked as though he was experiencing some hard times. He confided in me that he was, for the most part, homeless. His clothing was filthy, and he looked as though he had not had an opportunity to shave or cut his hair for some time. He traveled from the West side to the South side whenever one of his lady friends or relatives was gracious enough to allow him to lay his head. We were in the midst of a profound conversation about life when my stop came, and we parted ways. My miracle twin nephews have been an inspiration on my pregnancy journey, a constant reminder that God would provide. A constant reminder that his will will be done, and he will show up in your darkest moments.

Deceit

At twenty-six weeks gestation, I went to a routine ob-gyn appointment and discovered that I had a slow leak in my amniotic sac. There was really nothing to do. The goal was to hold the baby in as long as possible. The next day, I ended up in a familiar broken place, the emergency room. This time, it would be okay, or at least I made myself believe that this time it would be okay. I had been reminded of my sister's situation last week on the train. Why wouldn't he come through for me? In my mind, I'd manifested this child, this baby girl that had to come to pass.

As life would have it, my amniotic sac broke. I began to experience contractions. I was in labor for several hours. My husband went home to stay with our son. There were many people who would have watched my son. Truthfully, I believe he went home because he could not handle another heartbreak. It was obvious to me that the miscarriage had taken something out of him. It's a topic that was never discussed. He maintained that it was no big deal, that he was okay.

That evening, I gave birth to a two-pound, five-ounce baby girl. She was extremely premature, but she was beautiful. I can honestly say that I was numb. The doctor came in to give the baby's prognosis. I had already known that she was early and that she would have to fight to live in this world. The next twenty-four hours would determine whether she had the energy to fight.

The critical stage passed, and Chantel was still here. My son and husband came to the hospital to see the new baby in the neonatal unit. Life was good, and we could breathe again. The doctor explained to us that there would be major difficulties raising a premature child. Medical issues and the emotional roller coaster would be a common part of the process. In a few months, if all went well, our baby girl would be allowed to leave the hospital. It all seemed so real.

A representative from the Cook County Records Department came into the room. My husband and I signed the birth certificate. Chantel was assigned a Social Security number, and she was added to my husband's medical insurance. I officially had a daughter. I exhaled. I received calls from friends and family. Everybody was so happy; the joy was overwhelming. I was extremely tired from the excitement. My head had barely hit the hospital bed pillow when I went to sleep. After a long day, my son and husband went home elated with the intent of returning the next day to visit Chantel and me.

It is normal to be awakened every few hours in the hospital to have your vitals checked. I was not concerned at all when the nurse would enter and leave. I had been asleep for a few hours when I was disturbed. It was about 2:00 a.m. There was really no need to disturb me in the early hours of the morning. I turned as I felt a gentle stroke to my hair and a touch on my shoulder. I slowly turned over to find a beautiful smile awakening me. The young lady in the white jacket spoke so softly. She explained that she was the overnight resident on call in the neonatal unit. I struggled to fully awaken, focusing on the role she had just shared. I smiled. She must have been coming to update me on my beautiful baby girl.

"It's Chantel," she murmured softly. "Her skin is so thin and fragile." Her voice changed, and a tear appeared in her eye. "I know your family is excited about your arrival. She is having issues with her heart and will not live without life support. I know it's a lot to take in. I am so sorry. I will leave you to make a decision." I could not speak. I only nodded while she spoke as tears ran from my eyes. I sat in a blank stare as tears and snot ran uncontrollably at this point. I could not breathe. I could not feel. I could not think. I could not pray. I felt spiritually and emotionally dead. Through it all, I knew that I had to somehow get myself together. I was the support for my family. If I broke down, everyone around me would collapse.

The hospital chaplain came in to see me a few hours later. I begged him to leave the room. At that moment, God and I had nothing to discuss. I would not acknowledge his presence in the room, nor would I acknowledge the message he intended to deliver. I had to see for myself. I had no interest in the thoughts of the doctor or the chaplain. He eventually caught on and left. I rang the call bell and requested that the nurse wheel me down to the neonatal unit. I had to see Chantel. I had to touch my beautiful baby girl.

When I entered the neonatal room, it was evident that my arrival was expected. My tiny baby girl was lying in an incubator, attached to various monitors. They were right. Her pale, flimsy, translucent skin was burning. I looked away to discreetly wipe my tears and requested that someone call my husband. "He is already on the way," the nurse said. They wheeled me closer to the incubator where Chantel lay. They then detached her from the monitor and life support. They put her in my arms, and I stroked her tiny fingers. She took her last breath while I held her. I really couldn't explain it, but as her spirit left her little body, a huge part of me left with her. It had to be done. She was suffering immensely. The chaplain held my hands as I sobbed emptily.

They sent my husband into the grieving room while they prepared the body. Neither of us was clear on what they meant when they said they were preparing the body until the nurse reappeared with Chantel. She was no longer dressed in hospital attire. She had on a tiny, knitted two-piece outfit with a hat and socks to match. I am positive now that my husband did not fully comprehend what was happening. The nurse walked over to the sofa where we sat and attempted to hand Chantel to him. He held her and smiled until it registered that his new baby girl was a lifeless corpse in his arms. She looked very much like a doll. In shock, he released Chantel, tossing the corpse in fear. The nurse quickly caught the shell that once held his daughter. She was livid and asked him if he had lost his mind. "Yes," was the answer to her question.

There was nothing in our life toolboxes that could have prepared us for opening our hearts to a newborn daughter and grieving her death within seventy-two hours. The pain faded slowly, but somehow never disappeared. Maintaining my strength was difficult. I felt as if my display of strength, joy, and peace would set the tone to salvage the unity of my family. I held on to my husband, and we sat in a room with the lights off. He went home, and I returned upstairs.

Pushing through the pain, I got up from the bed later that same day. I sucked in my tears, dressed myself, and practiced my facade in the mirror. "You are okay," I repeated until it was a believable statement. I sat in a chair on the side of the bed. I had to leave sooner than later. This room was smothering me.

As I sat there, the chaplain entered. I smiled and spoke to him. He spoke politely and then asked to speak to the mother he'd met with earlier that morning. "I am her," I replied. I guess I had really built my poker face. The man of God didn't recognize me. About twelve hours before, as Chantel released her last breath in my arms, I was a distraught, angry, ugly mess. A few hours had not changed anything. Makeup and hair have a way of masking female emotions. He complimented me on my cleanup. We talked for a few minutes. I maintained that I was okay, and he at least pretended to believe me. People from various departments entered the room continuously. Half of them were still congratulating me, completely unaware that I was mourning the loss of my child. Each time, I was forced to verbalize the reality that Chantel had gone away just as quickly as she had come.

Chapter 6

AGAIN

There are no words to articulate my level of brokenness. In the midst of the hurt, I was also ashamed. Word had gotten out that I had finally had a baby. Very few people knew that she was gone. Gifts and congratulations were coming in from family, friends, and church members until someone spread the word that she was gone. People didn't know what to say, so they said absolutely nothing. I quickly went back to my routine, though it would be a few weeks before I would return to work. My time was spent ironing, cooking, and cleaning for my family. My son and husband never discussed what had happened. They got up each morning, went to school and work, seemingly moving on with their lives. They had to be hurting as much as I was. The tension in their presence was discomforting.

When I was alone, I crawled into bed, hugged my pillow, and cried uncontrollably. There are situations in life that will force your spirituality or cause you to question everything you've ever been taught. *Who is God anyway?* I thought. How is it that the same God who allowed my nephews to live sat by and watched as Chantel breathed her last breath in my arms? I had been a good girl, a good person my whole life, always choosing to make the choices that I thought to be the right thing to do. Of course, I am human, and I've made mistakes. I took ownership of my mistakes and apologized when I was wrong.

I grew up in an era when everyone around me was hanging out, engaging in promiscuous behavior, and using drugs. The spirit within me invoked a discipline that allowed me the strength to be a caregiver during those trying times. I gave of myself, pouring my spirit into healing others my whole life. All I wanted was for God to allow me an extension of myself.

Somehow, God managed to speak to me during my brokenness and loneliness. I was empty, yet I was full. I cursed God, yet I literally sang his praises. The pit of my soul pained, yet I poured out glory to his name. I wasn't intentionally doing this by any means. It was the way I coped. Having been raised in the church and around the remnants of the spirit, it was all I knew. Singing was so therapeutic. The words of the gospel music were soothing. I grew up listening to my grandmother sing. When she was happy, she sang. When she was sad, she sang. When she was discouraged, she sang. When she was so broken and sick of singing, she slid out a soothing yet powerful moan. Yet she sang.

As I attempted to turn my back on my Creator, he used the only tools I'd allowed to penetrate my psyche to hug me and rock me to sleep each night. Don't get it wrong. I had good and bad influences in my life. I had been exposed to the pits of hell while being protected by God's glory unknowingly. With free will in play, many situations could easily have been catastrophic. There were many in my personal and professional life who embraced my brokenness, making attempts to chip away at my wounded spirit. My ears would ignore many hurtful rumors spread by my family, including speculations of my married life and the way I couldn't hold a child, and the whispers of the neighbors as I attempted to move around and regain my sense of normalcy in my life.

After several weeks, I returned to work, my self-proclaimed sanctuary. I had been avoiding the first day back like the plague. The awkwardness of people, unaware of how to react to hardship, would inevitably present itself to me. That first day back, I wrapped myself in a beautiful garment and presented myself with my powerful, Godgiven strut. My team leader, a good associate, greeted me at the door. He sensed my discomfort and said something hysterically crazy to break the ice. I can't quite remember the words that came from his mouth. Whatever he said was so outlandishly funny that I let out a roaring burst of laughter as I entered the office door. Laughter is healing, though not necessarily in this instance.

As I belted out a roar of joy from the pit of my stomach, one of my coworkers blurted out, "What the hell are you laughing about? Nobody wants to hear that ——. Go back where you came from." Laughter quickly turned into tears. My only response to the unwarranted attack was to exit the office doors as quickly as I had entered. My team leader followed me out the door as other colleagues addressed the distraught woman. My team leader explained to me that the woman, my coworker, had recently lost her mother. She was not handling it well. She had chosen bitterness. He shook his head and then put his hands in his pockets.

Restoration came quickly. Two more of my coworkers now stood outside of the office door as though they had been prompted. One of them had an envelope in her hand. She presented the envelope which contained $100 and tickets to a comedy show. Ironically, I could enjoy a night of laughter with my husband. "It isn't much," she said. To me, it was everything. I was then sent home with pay to return the following week. Small tokens of love and kindness literally have the power to change a life. I had a conversation with my creator. I had asked for restoration, and he answered.

Unwarranted faith

Life eventually got back to our version of normal. I went back to work, my husband and son continued their daily routines, and I socialized with family and friends. Life continued as if nothing had ever happened. As time passed, the pain dissipated. My husband and I went back to intimacy with each other. It was different, though. We did use protection, and it was mutually intentional. He was my husband, and neither of us wanted the latest issue between us. The difference was my unsettling fear of becoming pregnant again. I was so frustrated. I was as fertile as a bunny rabbit. Would I ever be able to carry a child to term? Why couldn't I carry a child to term? What was wrong with me? The sadness that consumed me was overwhelming when thinking about the ambiguity in the answers to these questions. I still was crazy enough to believe that I could do it. That thought, passing in my spirit, was more overwhelming than the sadness. Some people thought I was a glutton for punishment. There were also humiliating rumors circulating regarding my inability to carry to term. People can be so unintentionally hurtful to mask their projection of another person's situation. Emotionally broken, I really didn't care what people thought; I was still on a quest, pressed to deliver.

Eventually, it happened again. Of course, we didn't tell anyone until I started to show. We were in the ultimate vulnerable state. We hid our joy, our pain, and most every other emotion for the sake of what other people feared for us. As soon as I discovered I was pregnant, I began to see a specialist. I was put on light duty and scheduled for a procedure to stitch my cervix closed at the beginning of my fifth month. The procedure wasn't supposed to be painful, but it was. Before the procedure, I was given a local anesthetic. As the doctor started to stitch my cervix, I could literally feel him sewing into my flesh like he was stitching a hem into a skirt. I began to squeal a sigh of pain. The doctor stopped and requested that the anesthesiologist give me more medication. The doctor and the anesthesiologist battled it out. The anesthesiologist was hesitant to give more anesthesia. I was in a twilight state. Apparently, giving more anesthesia would put me to sleep and jeopardize my life. I found myself in another life-threatening situation. Eventually, the anesthesiologist agreed; however, he and his team had to stay in the room for observation during the whole procedure.

The procedure went well. Most importantly, I woke up. I kept my activity to a minimum. I still walked frequently because it was necessary. I was still working. I caught public transportation at times. The doctors didn't see anything wrong with the movement until it happened. I began to leak a pink discharge. He was so hopeful, so I maintained faith. He warned that there might be complications. We were hopeful that the discharge would stop.

I decreased my activities, only moving around when necessary. I still went to church every Sunday. The choir director still voiced her opinion out of concern. She simply couldn't understand why I kept putting myself through this anguish. "We're going to name this baby Christina," she said. "When you have this baby, that will be her name." I came to a deeper realization that the people around me were both faithful and tired of mourning about my situation at the same time.

About two weeks passed from the time that I'd had the procedure. I felt okay and appeared to be in good spirits. I wasn't sure what would happen. Experience had taught me that it would be okay, regardless of the outcome. I prayed more than anything that I would have a healthy child and that I would be mentally, physically, and emotionally sound.

Emotionally drained

I sat in the labor and delivery room pondering the thought: *Is there any possibility that this child could be healthy?* I started spotting, then found out that my body had rejected the cerclage. I was about twenty-five weeks pregnant and in labor. Chantel had taught me not to be selfish and to turn off my emotions. Immediately, my grandma Mary came to mind. "Put your feelings in your pocket and sit on them," she would say. "That's exactly where they are most effective." Decisions made out of pure emotion are generally unwise.

The doctor came in and informed me that his team would not be able to stop the contractions. To add to the situation, midway through the labor process, I was informed that there was no heartbeat. That evening, I delivered Christina. This time, I was alone. I had to endure another D&C. At least I had anesthesia. I was in unbearable pain. I was given Demerol to soothe the pain, but the pain persisted. I was then given morphine. Until this incident, I had no idea that I was allergic to morphine. My skin broke out in hives, and I felt like I was on fire from the inside and had no way to calm the flames. I was given gloves to put on my hands to keep me from literally tearing through my skin. I was finally restrained until the Benadryl or whatever medication they gave me started to work in my body. I was so disoriented with all the medication. I had never taken drugs in my life. Whatever they were giving me was not working, and I acted a pure fool.

Later that evening, I was given another series of drugs to stop the allergic reaction and calm my aching body. I don't think there was a drug invented that could ease the hurt and the anguish that I endured. Far beyond the sting that pierced through my skin and the aches that perforated through my body were the emotional scars, wandering thoughts, and emptiness. The nurses were absolutely amazing. They laughed and joked with me even in my intoxicated state of mind. When I came to myself the next day, my bed was filled with baby paraphernalia—socks, rattles, pacifiers, the works. Apparently, someone had not gotten the memo and came bearing gifts. The nurses turned an emotional situation into something hilarious. I couldn't really remember most of their antics. I only remember words of encouragement and them putting the diapers and onesies on their heads and dancing. I had to pump milk to ease the pain in my breasts. I was lactating—a reality that my milk had street value, enough opiates to lay a heroin addict flat. Again, we laughed.

Strangely, though this was a horrific situation, it was somehow therapeutic. God will send his angels to lift you during your brokenness, so long as you're receptive to healing. Life always gives us a plethora of options, the choice to experience joy amidst difficulty. Some choose to wallow in self-pity and feel defeated. I choose joy. I could have easily given into anger and hate, but God…

Chapter 7

UNFOLDING THE TRUTH

This is not meant to be a somber story. The purpose is to display that resilience is necessary to progress through life's trials and tribulations. Just like bringing about life in pregnancy, it is necessary to deliberately push through obstacles to reach the jewels that life has to offer. Tears, the mist that left the tips of my eyes. The many judgments I had to lay to rest. Forgiveness of many grudges in need of being released. Overwhelming sorrow dissipated from my cheeks, running down my neck. The ugly cry, the kind that the elders see as disgraceful.

Oblivious to my surroundings, I focused on my pain and how to release it, how to truly heal so I could move on. I had no clue as to what I was moving on to. I only knew that it was imperative that I move. Sitting stagnant would literally suffocate my hopes, my dreams, my visions. At that moment in time, being still would have robbed me of my life.

I was wholeheartedly progressing forward when I returned to work for about six months. I was amazed at the work that my team was doing in the projects. The plan for transformation, which was a plan to disband most public housing happened to be on what was now considered prime property in Chicago, was being implemented, whether the residents liked it or not. We spent a lot of time in the Ida B. Wells housing complexes. Many were afraid to enter these communities, but I wasn't—I was coming home, having spent the first thirteen years of my life in Ida B. Wells public housing.

I felt an inner peace from having come full circle, though there was some sadness. The presence of our team was tangible evidence that the projects were coming down. The residents were in deep denial, understandably so. There had been years of discussion about demolishing public housing and replacing the dilapidated structures with chic new mixed-income housing. After all, most public housing complexes in Chicago were a straight shot to downtown, offering the best views of the architecture and the most transportation options.

I have my own views on mixing middle-class residents with multigenerationally low-income families without changing the mindset of the people. On its face, I guess it makes sense—at least to the politicians it did. If poor people lived around middle-class people, the poor people would be inspired to work to acquire a similar lifestyle. Realistically, it was a dangerous idea. Yes, a small percent of the population would be inspired to find employment or get training. The larger group would hold resentment toward their neighbors who were living well because of a mindset that had been embedded in a people and passed on from generation to generation, a mindset brought about by social entitlement. Entitlements, supposedly initially meant to be temporary—a hand-up—became progressively permanent and a handout. Here we were in the trenches, some of the most dangerous public housing developments in the country, attempting to convince Social Security disability recipients that they should find employment and eventually give up their *sure-thing* checks.

I was enthusiastic about my message because I did it. If I was able to do it, get an education, and find a career that I loved, anyone could. Most residents were excited until it was mentioned that if their income became substantial, they would have to give up their subsidies including food stamps, Social Security, Section 8 rental assistance—all of these were deal-breakers. The residents began to talk. Most thought I was too far removed from my situation to empathize with theirs. I had made it out of the Ida B. Wells before the New Jack City era when most residents were held hostage in their homes due to gangs literally taking control of the housing development.

A young lady I played with as a little girl now worked with one of the community partners. We reminisced about how we used to play Red Light-Green Light, hide-and-go-seek, and double Dutch in the courtyards. She went on to talk about how the same young boys that we played Catch a Girl Kiss a Girl with had turned into vicious young men. As violent gang members, they would drive down the street shooting automatic weapons. They would stand on the rooftops, terrorizing the community and acting out Hollywood's portrayal of a violent, desecrated Black community. She talked about the hopelessness and the fear: being afraid to send your children to school, being afraid to go outside to get groceries, let alone sitting on the stoop and laughing with neighbors. Yes, it was a violent time that I had escaped.

From that aspect, they were right. I was unapologetic that I had missed being held captive in my home, and I was sad that some had PTSD from the experience, yet others glorified it. Our people perish for lack of knowledge, scripture from the Bible, Hosea 4:6. We have a responsibility to educate all who are willing to drink from the proverbial fountain.

We recruited a young man who was known in the public housing. He had gone to college on a basketball scholarship. He somehow injured his knee, which ended his basketball career and his education. Initially, he took a temporary job as a spokesman for the money. He had no belief in the program at all. They had been talking about tearing down the projects for years. In his mind, it would never happen. After all, four generations of his family had been raised on this land. His reality kicked in when he stayed away from the neighborhood for a few weeks. He met us at the office on the West side one day, and then we all rode to the Wells together.

As my supervisor turned the corner to enter the community, the young man began to cry. Demolition machines were on the property and had torn down structures that had been there a few days before, the destruction of what was people's homes. He became diligent about becoming knowledgeable of resources, passing all that he learned to the residents of the community. There is no way to tell how many people benefited from the program long term. Many people worked a job for a few months and then quit in fear of losing their benefits. Others started academic programs and training programs that were ongoing when our program ended. Ironically, our program lost funding. I was offered a layoff, and I accepted it. I smile as I reminisce.

Years later, I saw that young man who helped me to help others. He saw me as I was coming out of my office building. At this point in my life, I had met so many people, I had no idea who he was. Mind you, my being visually impaired could also have been the issue. As he jarred my memory, I was overwhelmed. He had enrolled in school when his job ended. He was working in social services and in graduate school. If the time that I spent at that job was only meant to touch somebody as I passed along on my journey, he let me know that my purpose was fulfilled. Maybe unintentional, purposeful deeds beget blessings. Maybe every experience we have and every connection we make is intentional, regardless of the benefits or the pain attached. Maybe every moment of our life holds a lesson, not necessarily for us, but eventually for the glory of our creator and his kingdom.

Coming out of the dark

You heard me right; I accepted a layoff after all that talk about keeping it moving. I got a revelation that I was moving too much, crazily enough, in the wrong direction. My body, mind, and soul were in deep need of rejuvenation. The time had come to bring calm to the tidal waves that I called life. Income was important, so of course, my first stop was at the unemployment office. As I have mentioned before, temporary subsidies—*hand-ups*—have the capability of changing the whole trajectory of your life. My husband was definitely in agreement with me taking some time off. Life experiences have changed me. It had changed all of us. The thought of calm in the midst of the storm was refreshing and beneficial to all parties, especially for me in my life. My getting back to myself meant more opportunities for them to receive home-cooked meals with all fresh ingredients. When I was mentally at ease, I would cook every day, and I did it well. One of my biggest pleasures in life was providing delicious meals and hosting parties for my family and friends.

It was midsummer. As I looked in the mirror and acknowledged the change in my body, I was frustrated. The weight from my past experiences had caught up with me. Remnants of each pregnancy weighed on my tired body. Don't get me wrong, I still had swag now. My attire became more free-flowing to hide the weight in my stomach. Each pound carried a memory—hurt and pain that must be removed in order for me to heal. Essential to moving forward, I joined the local gym, hired a personal trainer, and enrolled my son in the taekwondo classes that were offered. My trainer was serious about the assignment. There were many times over the next year that I just didn't feel like being bothered. She would literally lay on my doorbell and blow up my telephone until I responded. I told her what the goal was, and she understood the assignment. She was going to hold me accountable. I enjoyed that time with my gym family. My major focus in life was healing. My mind, body, and soul needed rest. I was free.

While in the gym in the morning and the afternoon, I found myself curious. No matter what time I showed up, the gym appeared to be full of people, the same people. I wanted to know: what do they do for money? I was surrounded by entrepreneurs, authors, business owners, etc., all in the gym rejuvenating and healing. Self-care is a luxury that most neglect to pencil into their busy schedule.

Self-care is a means of wealth and prosperity. Think about it. As humans, we perform better when we are healthy, focused, and wellrested. Working with a trainer taught me to push through the pain. The end results are far more beneficial than the moment your brain acknowledges your body's breaking point, triggering a sensation that either prompts you to stop or pushes you forward. When we manage to experience the other side of the threshold of pain, the options are limitless.

Defeating obstacles becomes strategically achievable once the key to surviving the pain is discovered, and conquering the technique can be duplicated whenever necessary. I managed to push through fifty pounds that year. Each pound represented a burden, a trial, or an obstacle that sat buried within me, waiting to resurface. With each weight pushed, I tore down a wall, acknowledging that life happens. Eventually, a different set of burdens will surface and accumulate. I was unconcerned; I had found the key.

The rediscovery of me

Gracefully broken and masterfully redeemed, I managed to find myself that year. You could say that I "got my swag back." I felt comfortable in my body and my skin. My walk was amplified, and my voice was unmuted. I started to unleash a small morsel of the power within me. I was beautiful, confident, and fierce. I realized that I was enough.

I began renovating everything. With the help of the most talented carpenter I know, I rehabbed our condo room by room. I started by stripping ten layers of paint from the red oak fireplace, restoring it to its natural beauty. The dining room was redone, floor to ceiling, in cobblestone. It mirrored the royalty of an Egyptian pyramid. The kitchen was done in black marble. Then, on a slim budget with beautifully discounted materials, I marveled at the newly found comfort.

It had started as a seemingly small task. The project actually ended up taking me fourteen months. There were many ups and downs. Several times I thought that the project would not be completed. Regardless of the obstacle, I never wavered in my faith. I persevered and the results were, *man, amazing!* To see something manifest itself from your mind into this world is a true miracle. This was the first time I had paid attention to manifestation in my life, the ability to envision and capture beyond what is in plain sight.

This idea is portrayed in spoken word:

> Spirit of the universe, hear my plea.
> These hands I've been dealt are bothering me.
> This road seems so hard and somber at times.

But the harder it gets, the farther I climb.
Determined, I know I can conquer this plight.
If I can identify the problem, I know I can fight.
Spirit of the universe, help me to see,
To find the problem, I must examine me.
This journey is causing me to grieve.
To let go of all that I used to be.
Everything I did was completed by sight.
Robbed by circumstance, I still must fight.
Spirit of the universe, I've made a decision.
I'll tear down each wall with great precision.
My journey is causing a rediscovery of me,
Not who somebody thought I was supposed to be.
I'm defined by my vision, not by my sight.
My destiny is gleaming as the sun is bright.
Catapult me into the sky, my dreams, my destiny.
Manifestation of a repeated vision that keeps on haunting me.
Like an eaglet thrust from a cliff, no choice but to fly.
I know I'm safe in your arms. I may fall but I won't die.
If I'm falling, you'll swoop me up and thrust me off the cliff again.
Faith—evidence of things unseen. Victory, I win.
Spirit of the universe, you heard my cry. I am finally free.
My hopes, my dreams, my vision, the rediscovery of me.

The difficulties that we endure, regardless of their significance, test our ability to persevere. These struggles bring about strength and the power to push forward to the other side, the things that we envision in life.

Chapter 8

SHOOTING ANOTHER SHOT

My church family

Stronger roots are essential to the ability to persevere. Haters are definitely going to hate. With the multiple naysayers in our lives, it helps to have a circle of friends that supports your ideology that the seemingly impossible is possible. That group for me was the members of First New Bethany Missionary Baptist Church. I was born into affiliation with this church, and I will die with the affiliation to this church. The many ways God saved me are captured within the aspects of this church and the hearts of its members. Each time I hurt, they took the blows with me. We sang, we praised, we prayed. Most importantly, we loved. Standing in the gap, sharing knowledge and wisdom that encourages the people around us to get up, shake off the spirits of discouragement, depression, and underachievement, dream big, and work to achieve your goals. You will be victorious; you have no choice but to be.

A small church congregation of about forty active members it is. Members who migrated from the South, Mississippi, to be exact. Business owners, principals, lawyers, actors, bankers, and history makers. One member of the church was the first Black woman to hold the title of principal within the Catholic School system, and another was the first of any race to drive a bus for the public transit system. They all prayed for me in the church. My support system leading this awesome group was the first lady and the pastor. Mother and father to the congregation, they exuded unconditional love, joy, and peace. They loved each of us as though we were theirs. There was no pretense; they were real. The messages were grounded in the word and offered timely wisdom for our current life situations. Their flaws were never hidden. They used the mishaps in their lives as lessons. I learned so much from them.

The banner that hung in the sanctuary read, "Work while it is day, for night cometh when no man can work" (John 9:4–5). It took a while for this message to kick in. I get it now: we don't know the time or the day when our daily routines will come to a halt. Work a meaningful, purpose-filled day in preparation for a time of stagnation. The first lady could tell your entire story from looking at you. It was hard to hide your pain and your fears from her. She knew that for whatever reason, I was determined to give birth to another child. I knew that she would support me through the process. As long as I had a vision, she interceded in prayer. Some don't believe, but the prayer warriors at First New Bethany, baby, their God is God.

Reflections of family

To date, I don't believe that my sisters and mother fully understood the rationale behind my determination to have another child. I knew that this process was painful. They were more concerned with me being alive than with me having another child. The situation was stressful, and they wished that I would rejoice in the son I had and move on with my life. "Maybe it wasn't meant to be," they would say. After several incidents, I don't blame any of them for being discouraged. The constant grieving was enough to harden anyone's heart against the idea of me conceiving another child.

My relationship with my husband looked great from the outside. We portrayed the American dream, minus the part where you have 2.5 children, of course. In the privacy of our bedroom, things changed. I loved him and he loved me, as much as we knew how at that time. Limited communication to address the hurt became a physical wall that lay between us in our bedroom. I had chiseled the perfect body, or so I thought. He complained that I had become too thin. My outer beauty was admired by many. The only man I cared to take a compliment from was my husband. He was the only affection and intimacy that I craved. That part of my marriage seemingly passed away bit by bit with each attempt at childbirth.

It may sound insensitive, but I was too caught up in my own agenda to nurture the wounds. I had no idea how to begin to express how I felt and what I envisioned. In many aspects, I felt like a failure. I never took more than a moment to dwell on it. The one simple task given to a woman that could not be completed by a man was the one that I could not fulfill. I could not carry a child in my womb. My husband never verbalized it, but he wanted another child. He could not understand what was so difficult. He had no clue what the medical terminology meant. All he knew was that it hurt. It was a recurring pain that he held in. Each time he got his hopes up, he was disappointed.

Every so often, we came together to make love through the pain. It wasn't the same. I didn't feel it would be the same until I was successful in bringing forth a healthy child. My son was young at the time. His life was filled with multiple cousins to keep him entertained. It was easier for me to believe that he was unbothered by my situation. This situation interfered with the dynamics of his family structure. My son was wonderful, though. As long as I was okay, he was okay.

Deeper faith

A few years had passed. Time had started to build a scab on the physical and emotional wounds that had disrupted our lives. I was in the best physical shape of my life. I had dedicated some time to myself and my family and had developed new friendships. These were non-biased people who had limited knowledge of the trauma I had endured. It was refreshing to meet new people and to feel whole. I met this group through a neighbor. She was always on a health kick and always looking for new business ventures. I had refused many offers from her to attend demonstrations for various products. On this particular day, she invited me on the spur of the moment, and I said yes. I jumped into her truck and rode with her to a friend's house for an informational meeting about Oriental-based health food supplements.

Upon arrival, I was amazed by the home. I absolutely love architecture, specifically Greystone structures. We pulled up to the most beautiful single-family structure. I expected nothing from the presentation. My focus was on admiring every amenity in the turn-of-thecentury restoration with stained glass windows and vaulted ceilings. The hand-carved crown molding was initially way more important than whatever they were talking about. It sounded like a multilevel sales pyramid. The owners of the home boasted about their ability to purchase the home due to the product sales. I was plenty impressed by the actual structure and couldn't care less how they purchased it. Nope, I was not participating in a pyramid scheme.

I started to tune in as the testimonials began. First, I listened to three women who swore by the products. They talked about their bouts with diabetes and cancer. They gave heartfelt testimonials about the energy and healing received from consuming the products. I was fascinated by the reported healing from these Oriental herbs. During the testimonials that were occurring in the middle of the most beautifully decorated living room, a woman stuck her head into the room and asked if one of the gentlemen would assist her. She returned with the most adorable set of twins. The man followed behind her with a portable playpen.

After setting the children in the playpen and making sure that they were entertained, she came to join the discussion. She talked about her struggle with depression and suicidal ideations which stemmed from having multiple miscarriages. She began to cry as she spoke about one of the products. She praised the product's assistance with helping her to carry her twins to term. I was suddenly intrigued. I grabbed all the literature that I could get my hands on. I researched the company, reading about the various herbs and ingredients used in the products. The product was moderately expensive. My husband had very little to say about the product. In his opinion, we had nothing to lose. "Go ahead and try it," he said.

My mother and sisters thought I was crazy. "Your neighbor is using you. She wants you to spend your money so that she can move up in the company," they said. I had made up my mind before I ever discussed the product with them. I was going to try the product to see if the herbs had the ability to heal my body, enabling me to carry a child to term. I spoke to my doctor. After reading the ingredients, he at least agreed that the herbs wouldn't hurt me. I purchased a month's supply of the product and took it every day as recommended. After a month, I felt as though I had more energy. Some people thought I was delusional. I know my body, though. I felt much better.

I purchased another month's supply from my neighbor and consumed it. She understood that I had no interest in selling the product. She knew my end goal, and she was all in. She started to purchase the product with her discount, giving it to me at cost.

With little effort, I found myself pregnant again. As soon as I missed my cycle, I ran to the doctor. He immediately put me on bed rest. *Here we go again,* was probably what they thought. I can't really say this time was different. Hell, each time was different. This time I was different. I was disciplined. I had learned how to say no. Several compromises had possibly interfered with my progress in the past. I had learned to say no to my family when they would ask me to go shopping. We were the epitome of shopaholics. We had never found a problem that buying a good shoe or an outfit wouldn't fix. Previously, I would walk around the mall with my sister until I got tired. When I got tired, she would push me in a wheelchair. I rationalized that the shopping outings were therapeutic and good exercise. I will never know if the trips impacted my pregnancy. I knew that however convincing they would be, the answer this time would be no.

Before, I consumed unhealthy foods and took my vitamin supplements when I remembered. I had become healthier and more regimented. I had the ability to consume healthy foods and follow a plan given to me to the letter. Everything has a purpose. Previously when I was pregnant, with the doctor's consent, my husband and I had sex about twice a month as long as the process wasn't painful. This time I had been given strict orders by the specialist: no stimulation, no penetration. It was surprising that I was able to conceive this time around. My husband and I had sex probably once every two months. He had limited interest, at least with me. I had lost my craving to make love to him out of necessity. The alternative would hurt too much. I never concerned myself to worry about where he was being satisfied. He had a high sex drive like myself, and I knew if he wasn't getting it from me, well, you know how that goes.

I ignored him coming in late at night. I ignored the smell of cigarettes on his body and the lipstick on his shirt collar. It wasn't because I didn't care. I was a young proud woman, raised by a proud woman. I didn't feel it was necessary to confront a grown man with his iniquities. I had things to do. I had a house to run and a family to keep together. My grandparents had been married for about sixty-five years at this time. For me, marriage was "till death do us part." Fortunately, I was not a murderer. Seriously, I figured like everything else in life, I would work it out. At any rate, it would not be complicated to obey the doctor's orders as it related to intercourse. Mysteriously, preparation for this journey had been laid out before its occurrence. The outcome was seemingly on me and my obedience. My job was to be obedient as I allowed my steps to be ordered and maintain discipline through this long, lonely process.

Chapter 9

THE ULTIMATE JOURNEY

Spiritual awakening

I was eight weeks pregnant and ordered to go on bed rest. I was allowed to go to church on Sundays and to the clinic every Thursday at noon. This would be a tedious task. I would have to figure out what my family would eat and how the house would operate without me. Generating a budget and paying bills from the bed wouldn't be difficult; it would actually give me something to occupy my time. I was not big on watching television, so I would need activities to stimulate my mind. We gathered books, pens, and paper and set them on the dresser so they would be easily accessible. The first examination after bed rest confinement went off without a glitch. After all, there wasn't much to detect: I was healthy, and the baby was intact. We got food while we were out and returned home.

My husband had changed his work shift so that he could take me to the clinic. He rotated turns with my sister and my mother. My son would come home from school and flop down on my bed. I would help him with his homework, then we'd watch TV or play a game of cards. He was twelve years old and an amazing child, easy to please, and rarely complained. He loved to eat, so he frequently watched me in the kitchen. It was time for him and his dad to bring their game when it came to preparing food. They had a few good meals, which they rotated throughout the month.

Admittedly, the journey was starting out great. I enjoyed being waited on. Generally, I always played the role of the hostess unless it was a special occasion. These guys had actually given me a bell. I was instructed to ring it whenever I needed something. This amazing treatment lasted for about a month before it slowly dissipated. After a while, my situation normalized. My husband went back to hanging out late, and my son spent more time hanging out with his cousins. I was left alone, eager for Thursdays and Sundays to come around.

Sunday was my day of peace. I had an opportunity to fellowship with my church family and sing in the choir. The connective way I praised was to make a joyful noise. I absolutely loved the opportunity to uplift the congregation. Participating in the choir became my refuge. The heart of my sanity was my praise. I don't believe that I ever verbalized to my church family that I was pregnant again. Pregnancy being one of the few things in life that exposes itself within a relatively short period of time, I figured they would eventually figure it out. Of course, eventually, they did. I was five months pregnant, and my stomach was huge. I was still taking the supplements. It may have been psychological, but in my mind, I felt better than I had felt in a long time.

Like passive Southerners, no one really said anything to me to address my pregnancy. They whispered among themselves, becoming quiet when I walked past. I actually appreciated them not asking questions because I had no response to give. I had no idea why I was doing anything at this point; I was being led by the spirit. I thought I was losing my mind. I was making a huge sacrifice.

Becoming acclimated to this situation was hard as hell. I was used to moving around, even in the church. I lived to dance although most thought I didn't know how. *Was it really worth it?* I asked myself. I would never have said it out loud. I thought about it frequently for a while though.

Eventually, I would refocus. No goal is attainable without positive thoughts and progressive actions.

My favorite part about Sundays was going to my grandmother's house after church. I would sit on the couch with my grandma. She wouldn't allow me to move past the couch unless I was going to the bathroom. I had better not stay in the bathroom for more than ten minutes. Someone would send my son or another member of the search party to check on me. We socialized while we enjoyed Grandma's cooking. The menu changed every Sunday, and I was excited. We had greens, green beans, squash, macaroni and cheese, dressing, chicken, pot roast, peach cobbler, homemade soup, and succotash. You name it, mama knew how to prepare it, and it was never disappointing.

After supper, we watched a little television, and my mom would drop me and my son back off at home. My saving grace was the extra food that my granddad would pack up for me to nibble on through the week. They didn't have much, but their actions always showed how big their hearts were.

I was confused about a lot of things throughout my life. I was never in question of their love for me. I rationed my winnings through the week, eating my grandma's food in between the meals that my men prepared for me. Each bite tasted like heaven and was a reminder of the sacrifices we make for our children. The love that a woman pours into a meal exemplifies the love she pours into her family. It was nourishment, as well as a reminder that everything would be alright.

Spiritual encounter

Now I was about six months along and feeling more comfortable. This was the longest I had ever carried a child since I had my son. My doctor was cautiously optimistic. It was more likely that the child would live now, but we were not out of the woods yet. My prayer, all of our prayers, were for a healthy child. This was not the time to get comfortable or stray away from the plan. It was time to hold steady and maintain discipline.

They say that just as you're about to receive your breakthrough, the enemy blocks the door with a series of obstacles. My fists were balled up and swinging toward the door, and then…

Whomever they were, they were not lying. All kinds of obstacles came my way. The temptation was real. "Can I get some?" he said.

"Some of what?" I responded. I wasn't eating anything as I lay hot and nearly naked in the bed. It was the beginning of July, and it was hot as hell. We loved our condo, but there was no central air, one of the reasons that we were moving.

He rolled on top of me and looked me square in the eye, then said, "You know what some is. It's been a long time."

In the back of my head, I reminded myself, *No stimulation,* moisture on my panties. *Whoops! Stimulation!* I thought. This shouldn't be happening. He hadn't tried to touch me in months, and I was okay with that. I would be lying if I said I did not want it. I craved his touch. This was beyond difficult. I needed to make a split-second decision. If I decided to give in to my husband, to make love to the man whose seed I was carrying, I would jeopardize the seed, the seed that we had consensually sown together and agreed to nurture to its full maturation. Yes, it would likely live outside of the womb at this point, but one night's pleasure could consequently cause months in the hospital attached to cords in an incubator with possible brain damage or developmental delay. Remember, the prayer was for a healthy child. I gently looked away, giving him the indication to get off me. He turned in anger and went to sleep. It was a necessary choice, the right choice. I didn't blame him. It was in his nature. Mental note: Lord, thank you for not making me a man. Difficulty thinking with the right head.

I thought the worst was over. Nope! Every store was having Christmas in July sales. My youngest sister swore that I was well enough to go shopping. We had baby stuff to buy. She was right, in a sense. We hadn't purchased anything, and we had refused all baby gifts to this point. We were not sure of the outcome, so we erred on the side of caution. I thought for a moment that it would be great to get out of the house. She could definitely push me in a wheelchair. I reflected back on my past shopping trips gone wrong. It was a hard no. I wasn't going to be able to do it. We've come too far. I get it. The excitement was in the air. My mother has seven grandsons, my sister has seven nephews. I was carrying the spirit of a little girl, and my little sister was ready to celebrate. She could see the finish line.

Unfortunately, the race wasn't over. I held to the plan, not leaving the house until Thursday. The specialist had asked me about my activities the next week. I told him about the challenges that had occurred in the previous week. He smiled. "This always happens. This is why I told you to maintain discipline. People get comfortable and mess up." The orders were the same.

When Sunday came around, I went to church as usual. I had no way of knowing that this particular Sunday would impact the rest of my life. The service was absolutely amazing. The pastor delivered a dynamic message as usual. The choir sang out of their hearts. Sister Barber sang, "I'll Go If I Have to Go by Myself." Her voice was powerful, echoing all of her emotions each time she sang.

After the invitation, the pastor initiated an anointing and prayer service. He called me up to the front. As I sat in the chair in front of the altar, I cried. The prayer warriors prayed so hard that day you could literally feel the spirit moving through the room. When the service was over, I sat in the back of the room waiting for my family. The pastor came up to me and gave me a hug, then he spoke and said, "Do you believe God loves you?"

I responded, "Yes."

He then said, "You don't have to come to church and sing in the choir to prove your love to him. I don't want to see you in this church anymore. If I don't ever see you again, don't come back to this church until you have that baby, and I mean it." The pastor had called me out. He said what he meant and meant what he said. There would be no more Sunday escapes. I would only be going to my Thursday appointment and returning home. This is what I had been ordered to do in the first place at my last appointment. I had made the exception myself and acted as if it was written into the plan to have another Sunday outing.

The birth of an angel

Now I lay here in this bed, almost seven months pregnant. My only escape was my Thursday appointments, which I looked forward to as much as I dreaded. I looked forward to the socializing, of course. The people around me were excited about the baby girl's arrival yet distanced themselves from what I dreaded: the unknown. We were all so hopeful this time that our prayers would be answered. My aunt had started to bring items that belonged to her daughter. She came to the door with my cousin's beautiful wooden rocking cradle, though I had told her not to. "Girl, I'm not studying you. We need to get ready to bring this baby into the world," her West Indies voice so sweet yet demanding. She continued to set up the crib, regardless of what I said. Auntie had no doubts or concerns; she had left the past in the past. She had more faith than all of us. Obviously, I had the faith to continue to subject myself to this continuous vulnerability. It's quite possible that I had a bit of PTSD at this point. I was far enough along to have a healthy baby, but flashbacks of the many times I had to grieve still haunted me. Auntie reminded me to relax and coast the water. The days were flying by so slowly now.

I had actually conceptualized that there was a huge possibility that there would be a baby. I started to work on the perfect name for this long-awaited spirit. My family and I had gone through at least a hundred names. Everyone suggested naming this child after something or someone significant to them. This soul had been trying to release itself for years. The name needed to be meaningful; it needed to be unique, but not in a *made-up-name* type of way. I don't mean to offend those who think, *No, she didn't*—I love the creative names that we as people give our children. It's not like my name is common. I was just waiting on a name from God. He would tell me its significance, and I would be obedient, regardless of my opinion.

Now weeks had passed. My due date was fast approaching. I still had not received a name. I was overwhelmed that the house still wasn't ready. We had started on the house a few months before I conceived. We designed it, broke ground, and it still wasn't ready. My husband had been handling the deal since I'd been on bed rest. He kept telling me that he had it and not to worry. He sent me pictures via text about once a week, showing me the exterior being built. They had run over budget on the interior fixtures for the second time. They'd increased the price of the house by $100,000. My husband acted like he wanted this house as much as he wanted this baby. I was so over this house.

To add to my frustration, I had developed acid reflux. The only thing I was able to hold down was unsalted tortilla chips. Apparently, my gallbladder needed to be removed, an issue that I couldn't begin to address until we delivered this baby. We were hopeful that she would make her debut no earlier than three weeks from now. In the meantime, I was going to eat these tortilla chips. Every so often I tasted a little nibble of what my family was eating, knowing that it would come right back up 70 percent of the time. I need to try to hold in some nutrients though. Fortunately, the herbal supplements and prenatal vitamins stayed down. This baby was very active. I could feel her shifting in my stomach. It was almost time for her to come. We needed a name.

I asked God to give me a sign, and he did. The other day while I was watching one of my favorite romantic comedies, it came to me. Don't judge me—I absolutely love lovey-dovey movies. *Love & Basketball* is such a sweet portrayal of young love and its roller-coaster ride of controversies. Getting to the happily ever after seems partially impossible. It always ends up well, though—at least in the movies, right? It's not like I didn't know the names of the actors. I'd seen the movie at least five times. This time, as the credits rolled, a name popped out. I started searching for derivatives of the name.

I finally found the perfect name. I shared the name with my husband and my son. We loved it; everyone had an opinion. My mom and sisters weren't too particular about the name. It would grow on them. I told them that I would continue to search just to get them off my nerves. I had no intention of changing my mind. We liked it. God gave it to me and that's all that mattered.

The delivery

Now I found myself in my hospital bed in labor and delivery yet again, completely exhausted and filled with emotion. Getting here was such a wild experience. Yesterday, I went to my mom's house for a fall barbecue. The weather was absolutely perfect for early October— sunny and about seventy degrees. In Chicago, that is a major signal to fire up the grill. My cousin was in from out of town, which was another reason to celebrate. She is enlisted in the military and had made her home in Virginia a few years ago. The family got together at my mom's house after we had all visited my grandparents. The afterparty was everything, as per usual. "Ain't no party like a Pringle party," and that's the truth.

I know I was going against the doctor's orders, but I was due in three weeks, so please. There was nothing wrong at this point; I was simply changing locations where I threw my feet up on the couch. I sat and laughed, interacting with my family while they played cards and talked trash. We reminisced and ate good food. I was still having issues with my gallbladder, but I was eating the food. I didn't eat much, but yes, I did get some barbecue, and yes, I was afraid it was going to come back up.

I was sitting in the living room waiting for my little sister to take me home. Everyone was in the back, cleaning the kitchen and putting up the leftovers. I stood up to go to the bathroom. A gush of liquid poured from me, not from my bladder, but uncontrollably from my vagina. I immediately touched my belly to make sure the baby was moving. She was moving, I think. Hell, I don't know. I was afraid. I began to call for anyone. "Come here," I yelled, attempting to be calm. When my family came into the living room, I was soaking wet, standing over a puddle.

My cousin screamed with joy. "I'm going to be here to see the baby being born!" My mom and my sister were as nervous as I was, and like me, they were doing a poor job of hiding it. By the time my mom confirmed that my water had broken, my sister had gone to get the car. The car was so close to the house that it may have literally been on the sidewalk. "Girl, get in!" she screamed. I wobbled to the car and got in. She pulled off so fast that she left my cousin behind. We were riding down Stony Island, going about sixty miles an hour. As fast as I thought we were going, not much time passed before my cousin pulled up alongside us, yelling with her head partially out of the car window, "Push, push, push!"

When we arrived at the hospital, my cousin went to grab a wheelchair while my sister went to retrieve a nurse from the emergency room. The nursing staff moved surprisingly quickly, triaging me and moving me to an examining room. My doctor had been informed that I was at the hospital. In the meantime, I was assigned to the attending doctor in the emergency room. My cousin and my sister were sitting with me when he came in. He was the most handsome specimen I had ever seen in the form of a doctor, like someone off one of those hospital-based TV series.

"Damn," my cousin muttered under her breath. "Can you examine me?" We giggled like schoolgirls. As he examined me, my untimely acid reflux made its presence known. The barbecue had decided to make a reappearance. I was so embarrassed as I flooded the doctor with undesirable bodily fluids. He had the face of Blair Underwood and the body of Dwayne Johnson, "The Rock." My embarrassment dissipated as the doctor gently cleaned me up and reassured me that women often vomited on him in the emergency room.

Eventually, I was given a delivery room. There was no hurry. The fine doctor informed me that I had only dilated two centimeters. It was late at night. I was barely having contractions, but my doctor had ordered the staff to assign me a room and keep me under observation until he arrived in the morning. Dr. Ishmael and my husband arrived at the hospital room at about the same time. Dr. Ishmael's voice was filled with excitement. "It's time to have a baby," he smiled. My husband stood by the side of the bed, biting his nails—a sign that he was either nervous or lying. In this case, he was understandably nervous. We were so close, but anxiety was overtaking his emotions. Now it was 9:00 a.m., and I had only dilated three centimeters.

Dr. Ishmael was concerned that I was not dilating fast enough. He warned that he might have to order a shot of Pitocin to strengthen my contractions to avoid a dry birth. At 11:00 a.m., my contractions had not progressed, and he ordered the Pitocin. By noon, it had gone from calm to a state where I thought I was going to die. It felt like this kid was banging a hammer into my vagina every ten minutes. The monitor displayed waves, a diagram of my pain. The nurse asked if I wanted Dr. Ishmael to order an epidural. I was in terrible pain. I had heard things about epidurals that frightened me, though. For whatever reason, it was embedded in my head that I would be paralyzed if I received one. The nurse did her best to educate me on the advancements in medicine and the rarity of paralysis by epidural. I wasn't convinced. "Nope. I can handle the pain," I proclaimed.

When the doctor returned an hour later, my whole mindset had changed. The labor pains were overwhelming. I was willing to take anything to calm the pain. Now mind you, I have a very high tolerance for pain. This little girl was overwhelming me, and I needed drugs. The nurse saw I was in pain and said I had waited too long. I was dilating more rapidly now and couldn't have the epidural. I knew they were lying. I couldn't go another few minutes, let alone another few hours, in this type of pain. Dr. Ishmael agreed to give me a CSE, a combination of spinal and epidural. He explained that the half epidural would slightly calm the pain. I was dilating slowly but progressively. It was explained that I needed to be able to feel the urge to push.

Be careful what you ask for. Mind you, I was at a teaching hospital. About six interns entered the room. Dr. Ishmael asked if it would be okay for the doctors in training to watch, and I agreed. The attending doctor completed the formalities. We completed paperwork and she gave an overview of the procedure. Then we signed documents, primarily disclaimers. I sat on the end of the table with my back turned to the group of doctors. The anesthesiologist instructed me to sit very still as the doctor inserted the needle into my spine. My left leg flew up. I tried to remain calm as I alerted the doctor that my leg had moved. Crazy thoughts flew through my mind as the doctor asked me to confirm which leg had moved. *I'm going to be paralyzed,* I thought as I confirmed that it was my left leg. The doctor slowly withdrew the needle and then reinserted it. I held my breath and tried not to think until the doctor informed me that the procedure had been successfully completed. Finally, I was able to sit comfortably in the hospital bed.

As I sat peacefully, the phone rang. It was my mother on the other end. "Did you have that baby yet?" she asked softly. I could hear several people in the background. Instead of answering her question, I asked her where she was. I could hear the voices of church members in the background. It was around noon on Wednesday. It was odd to hear their voices in the background.

"What's going on, Mom?" I asked. She hadn't responded when I asked her where she was.

My stepfather took the phone from her and began to talk. "We're at the hospital," he said. "Pastor Tate had a stroke, and we're here. Don't worry about what's going on here. Did you have that baby yet?"

I took a deep breath and responded, "No." The call ended as I prayed.

I prayed that the pastor, the shepherd God had led me to, to feed me the word for a good portion of my life, would be okay.

Maybe an hour had passed since I had the procedure. The labor pains were back again like lightning. I'd dilated seven centimeters, and the contractions started to come much faster. When I reached eight centimeters, the doctor came into the room. My husband had also made his reappearance and turned on the television. The Chicago White Sox were playing the Boston Red Sox for the American League championship. "Wouldn't it be great if the White Sox went to the World Series?" they chatted.

"Wouldn't it be great if y'all were paying attention to me having a baby?" I growled.

The doctor rubbed my leg and proclaimed, "I'm paying attention. You're almost ready." It hadn't been long since the doctor had entered the room. In an effort to comfort me, he checked me again. I had dilated fully, and he was waiting for the baby to crown. "She's crowning," he said. "Wow, that's a lot of hair on this kid," he laughed. "Time to make your entry, young lady."

He paused, asking what the baby's name would be. "Sanai Cierra Fowler," I responded.

"Sanai," he smiled. "Arabic for love, truth, brilliance. That's a great name." He rubbed my leg. Her head was so hard. I gave a few good pushes, and she wouldn't come out. I pushed harder as directed, and she flew out and she ripped me. "Welcome, Sanai," he smiled as he began to check her vitals. She belted out a huge cry, and it was music to all of our ears.

So many years of trying to come into this world. The spirit that was named Sanai was finally here—success born from pure faith. The spirit of Sanai had finally found an appropriate vessel and graced the world with her presence. Words could not adequately explain how we felt when we looked at her for the first time. Now I lay here holding the most beautiful curly coal-black-haired little doll, skin the color of the milky caramel latte that my grandpa used to make us before lattes were overpriced at the local coffee shops. Her eyes were iridescent, the color of chocolate diamonds. I gazed into her eyes, unsure of what the future held for her. I only knew that she would be as brilliant and purposeful as her name. I knew, unequivocally, beyond a shadow of a doubt, that she was born through me, not just as a gift to me, but as a gift to the world. I understood the importance of her purpose, though it would only be activated with her full acceptance and consistency. She was by no means perfect, nor would she ever be. She was whoever her Creator designed her to be. Every trial and every obstacle in her life came as tools to be used or lesson to be learned. I am the guardian of an angel.

As her parent, I will love her, and nurture her, understanding that she is a gift. I will never idolize her, putting her on a pedestal. Her exalting will come from her Creator in her own time. I will teach her to be humble in her beauty and her gifts. She will know who and whose she is, with or without affirmation from man. Her path will be difficult. She will always have support. She will be open-minded, believing in the impossible. I give all honor to my Creator, Yahweh, Jehovah El Shaddai, Lord Almighty, for all that he has done and all that he is destined to do. The birth of Sanai is a testimony that you can have whatever you say. With faith, obedience, and discipline, all things are possible.

Chapter 10

LESSONS IN THE JOURNEY

Pushing through the pain

I would be lying if I told you that I would knowingly go through this again without first being guaranteed my desired outcome.

Of course, I would still desire to have a child. I would probably still feel the pressing need to bring forth a beautiful spirit that I now call Sanai. Had someone revealed to me, even in prophecy, that I would have a healthy baby with no delivery issues and then suffer two miscarriages, a stillborn child, and a child who would die in my arms, I would never have consciously chosen the pain. Who wants to be hurt? We spend our whole lives analyzing and assessing situations to determine the level of danger, pain, or risk we will endure before proceeding with any plan. When we imagine our life goals, our unfulfilled dreams seem so splendid, amazingly shooting straight to the top of whatever game we are in with no obstacles. What would drive you to get there, and what would motivate you to stay?

Think of the many celebrities and their children who were born rich. Mind you, there is absolutely nothing wrong with creating a legacy for your children and future generations. What happens when those children are not taught to respect others' lives and money? The journey becomes rugged, often leading to the same situations that their parents attempted to shelter them from: substance abuse, poverty, and depression. Obstacles and defeats in life give us the grit and grind needed to appreciate trying and to strive for the goals that we desire.

While on this journey, I often felt defeated, unworthy, and as though I was crazy to think that I could have another child. In my particular situation, my major conflict was obedience—obedience to the spirit within me and to the doctors around me who shared my goal and my dream. It was not until I removed the wants and needs of the people around me that accomplishing my goal became possible. The most overwhelming part of my journey was the initial inability to put the world on mute. I learned to filter out both the positive and negative views of those who have no direct relevance to a situation. This means disregarding the feelings of others' opinions toward your situation based on their importance. We are told all our lives not to be offensive. The journey has taught me that sometimes offense is necessary. Protect your goals, your hopes, your dreams, and your peace with your life. Develop the ability to discern spirits in each state of this journey called life. There is something to learn from each character, even those who are removed in the first scene. Learn your lesson without passing judgment and keep moving.

I will never forget an encounter I had when I was eighteen years old. I was sitting in the waiting room of the clinic, waiting for my turn to see the gynecologist. A woman disclosed to the nurse that she had six pregnancies and two children. When the woman left, the nurse stood in judgment of her, accusing her of having several abortions. Instead of minding my business, I engaged in the conversation, agreeing, "How can you be pregnant six times and only have two children without having abortions?" Documenting my journey, having been pregnant six times with two children, I have learned not to judge. More importantly, I've learned to immerse myself in my own journey while minding my own business.

Living in purpose

This is a topic that deserves more profound discussion. Have you ever really sat down and pondered the question, "Why am I here?" I had months to ponder the thought while on bed rest. The many wondrous ideas that went through my head were then interrupted by life. Now after lying dormant for many years, they rise. While lying in bed and lapsing into my purpose, I discovered that I was an author, an influencer, a motivational speaker, an employer, and a provider of housing. Somehow, when I got out of bed, the noise of the world—the need to be a good mother, a good wife, a good friend, a good daughter, and a good employee—prevailed. Though I did well in all of those areas, I made choices that sacrificed my purpose momentarily.

I made many decisions that, though I have learned many lessons from them, have prolonged my path to various destinations. Many doors have been closed due to complacency, procrastination, and fear. I have rationalized overstaying my welcome in professional and personal relationships. I won't say that I have wasted time, but I will definitely confess to delaying progress. The experiences that have accumulated are now to be shared for the uplifting and helping of others on a larger scale. All my life, we have been taught to work traditional jobs, take care of our closest family and friends, and keep our business to ourselves. At this moment, I declare that I continue to share intricate parts of my life to better the lives of others. I promote living in vulnerability as opposed to being afraid of embracing change. I'm pulling off layers unapologetically. I have finally muted the noise and am free to live the life that was given to me—a life that breathes life into others while radiating newly found energy.

All the experiences that could have potentially killed me saved me. I have discovered strength that I never knew was within me. Most importantly, I have discovered that the greatest love of my life is not my family, not my job, not myself. It is the Holy Spirit within that leads and guides me. When I step out of the way, my steps are ordered, and the greatness of my creator is delivered through me.

God's reward

The next time you're stepping off the curb and your inner voice pushes you back onto the sidewalk just before you feel the rushing wind of a speeding vehicle blow by, acknowledge that voice. This is generally the voice we refer to as intuition. Everyone has heard of this experience or a similar one. The thought of the near-death experience is brief and often unbothered. Imagine the ability to chime in on that intuitive voice in every aspect of your life. That voice within us is always there. How far would we progress, or how extremely different would we be if we tuned in just 50 percent more of the time? As we go through life, we can either ignite the voice, second-guess the voice, or allow outside parties to contradict it. What if it is true that everything needed to achieve your goals and dreams is literally within you? For the purposes of our creator, the gift is the ability to push forward life through the ability to discern the voice—the voice that generally attempts to assist you in subduing the seemingly unachievable or impossible. Going against the grain is considered to be a rebellion or crazy. What if more of us listened to that voice, risking being labeled as crazy in a culture where everything unpopular is considered taboo until it miraculously manifests itself into the latest technology or pop-up businesses?

Tuning in and focusing on that voice has always had the ability to change the world around us. Greatness lies within the voice. The answer to the question that every human asks, "Who am I, and why am I here?" is hidden within the voice. I will never again underestimate the voice that leads and guides me on my journey. I know I'm not perfect. No one is. I am exactly who my creator needs me to be, unapologetically. I urge you to manifest greatness into your life. Anything that is envisioned can be brought to fruition. You can have whatever you say exceedingly, abundantly, or more than you can ask or think in accordance to the power that is within you, a summary of Ephesians 3:20–21. It would behoove us to speak positively as opposed to negativity over our lives and the lives of others. The power of an abundant, meaningful life is within us. We have an obligation to our

Creator and ourselves to use the experiences that attempt to destroy us as positive tools for the uplifting of God's kingdom.

The hate, the anguish, the pain—surreal.
Words can't quite describe the way that I feel.
Out of breath, smothered, cardiac arrest.
Suffocating, held underwater, fighting to take a breath.
Gasping, fainting, crying for help, but no one can hear me
    scream.
The voice, the vision in my head, all of my smothered
    dreams.
Fighting desperately to be released before I go to sleep.
Depression, procrastination, emotional breakdown, and a
    counterproductive weep.
I tried lifting my eyes to the sky, a word fell down on me.
It hit like a bolt of lightning from a cloud and pierced really
    deep.
You're crying and screaming and fighting, wholeheartedly
    resisting change.
Promoting a different outcome while keeping things the
    same.
Self-sabotage at its best, a whirlwind of burning fire.
Sinking rapidly in quicksand and believing you're being
    lifted higher.
An oxymoron it may seem when you're young you think it's
    lit.
Doing your best to fit in, never rocking the boat, it seems
    legit.
Yelling, "Beam me up, take me away. Shit, this world is
    mine."
Living the same life, slightly rearranged and steadily wasting
    time.

You knock on every door, then before they open, you pivot
and run away.
Abandonment of your true self, yet you swear you're here
to stay.
You thought you could, they said you can't.
Neither matter until you did.
One day your ideas will be gone, permanently off the grid.
I awakened quite frantically, in a cold sweat.
My dreams, my goals, my aspirations—will they ever be
met?
Enlightenment, useless without implementation,
took a second to meditate on that.
I want to be empty when I take my final breath, pouring out
all I had to give.
Cultivating minds for generations, that's the only way I can
live.
Leaving this world doesn't bother me, forever will I stay.
You won't catch me buried wide awake,
a dormant seed in a watery grave.

ABOUT THE AUTHOR

Sherinda Pringle was born in Chicago. She spent the first thir- teen years of her life in the Ida B. Wells Homes, a public hous- ing complex, where she gained her edge. She spent her high school years in a small town north of Chicago, Zion, where a pleth- ora of positive and negative exposures carved out a rare diamond. Sherinda was born legally blind to a single mother. She gained her faith and wisdom through viewing life through the lenses of the peo- ple around her. Despite major difficulty seeing the words, Sherinda was an avid reader. Born from unique circumstances was a vivid imagination and the ability to use words to paint pictures.

Sherinda has a master's degree in community counseling. While in graduate school, she was told that she had the gift of insight. For more than a quarter century, she has used that gift to assist with heal- ing the broken and guiding the stuck into purpose-filled lives.

Sherinda uses her stories and poetry as a testimony that it doesn't matter what it looks like. God is…

RECLAIMING
YOUR
BOUNDARIES

A Transformational Journey to Confidence & Freedom

VOL I

Welcome to Your Path of Strength and Self-Respect

Congratulations! By embarking on this journey, you're taking a powerful step toward reclaiming your life, setting firm boundaries, and establishing the respect you deserve. Boundaries are not barriers—they are declarations of self-worth, guiding you toward healthier relationships, personal fulfillment, and professional success.

For the next 12 weeks, you will gain the clarity, confidence, and practical tools to define, enforce, and maintain boundaries in every area of your life. This workbook will serve as your personal guide, helping you identify patterns, overcome obstacles, and step into your most empowered self.

Why This Workbook Matters

Many women struggle with setting boundaries—feeling guilty, afraid of conflict, or unsure of where to start. If this sounds familiar, you're not alone. This workbook is designed to help you break free from these limiting fears and give you the exact strategies to:

- Recognize where your boundaries are weak and how to strengthen them
- Assert your needs without guilt or hesitation
- Navigate workplace and family dynamics with clarity and confidence
- Prevent burnout by balancing responsibilities with self-care
- Foster healthy, fulfilling relationships built on mutual respect

Week 1:
Introduction to boundaries

What does a boundary mean to you? Why are they essential for healthy relationships and personal growth?

_____

_____

_____

_____

_____

_____

_____

_____

_____

_____

_____

_____

_____

_____

_____

_____

_____

_____

Daily Journal

Week 2:
Experience with Boundaries

Date: _____

Reflect on moments when your boundaries were respected or violated.
How did each experience shape your emotions and self-worth?

_____

_____

_____

_____

_____

_____

_____

_____

_____

_____

_____

_____

_____

_____

_____

_____

_____

_____

_____

_____

Daily Journal

Week 3:
Identifying Boundaries at Home

How do family dynamics impact your ability to set boundaries? What shifts need to happen for a more supportive home environment?

_____

_____

_____

_____

_____

_____

_____

_____

_____

_____

_____

_____

_____

_____

_____

_____

_____

_____

_____

Daily Journal

Week 4:
Identifying Boundaries at Work

What workplace challenges make setting boundaries difficult? How can you confidently enforce limits with colleagues and supervisors?

_____

_____

_____

_____

_____

_____

_____

_____

_____

_____

_____

_____

_____

_____

_____

_____

_____

_____

_____

_____

_____

Daily Journal

Week 5: Communicating Boundaries Effectively

Date: _____

How comfortable are you asserting your boundaries? Learn powerful communication strategies that makes boundary-setting easier.

_____

_____

_____

_____

_____

_____

_____

_____

_____

_____

_____

_____

_____

_____

_____

_____

_____

_____

_____

_____

Daily Journal

Week 6:
Overcoming Guilt and Fear

What emotions hold you back from setting firm boundaries? Discover strategies to overcome guilt, fear, and self-doubt.

_____

_____

_____

_____

_____

_____

_____

_____

_____

_____

_____

_____

_____

_____

_____

_____

_____

_____

_____

_____

_____

Daily Journal

Week 7:
Balancing Work and Family Life

How do you currently balance personal and professional responsibilities? Identify changes needed for a healthier, more fulfilling lifestyle.

_____

_____

_____

_____

_____

_____

_____

_____

_____

_____

_____

_____

_____

_____

_____

_____

_____

_____

_____

_____

Daily Journal

_____

_____

_____

_____

_____

_____

_____

_____

_____

_____

_____

_____

_____

_____

_____

_____

_____

_____

_____

_____

Week 8:
Managing Cultural Differences

How do cultural norms shape boundary-setting? Uncover ways to navigate cross-cultural challenges while standing firm in your values.

_____

_____

_____

_____

_____

_____

_____

_____

_____

_____

_____

_____

_____

_____

_____

_____

_____

_____

_____

_____

_____

Daily Journal

Week 9:
Self-Care and Boundaries

How do you prioritize yourself without feeling selfish? Learn how self-care and boundaries work together for your well-being.

_____

_____

_____

_____

_____

_____

_____

_____

_____

_____

_____

_____

_____

_____

_____

_____

_____

_____

_____

_____

Daily Journal

_____

_____

_____

_____

_____

_____

_____

_____

_____

_____

_____

_____

_____

_____

_____

_____

_____

_____

_____

_____

_____

Week 10: Setting Boundaries with Technology

Date: _____

How do you manage work calls, emails, and social media without overwhelm? Take control of digital distractions and reclaim your time.

_____

_____

_____

_____

_____

_____

_____

_____

_____

_____

_____

_____

_____

_____

_____

_____

_____

_____

_____

_____

Daily Journal

Week 11: Boundary Maintenance and Flexibility

Date: _____

How do you sustain your boundaries over time? When is it okay to be flexible, and when should you stand firm?

_____

_____

_____

_____

_____

_____

_____

_____

_____

_____

_____

_____

_____

_____

_____

_____

_____

_____

_____

_____

_____

Daily Journal

_____

_____

_____

_____

_____

_____

_____

_____

_____

_____

_____

_____

_____

_____

_____

_____

_____

_____

_____

_____

_____

_____

Week 12:
Reflection & Moving Forward

Date: _____

What progress have you made in setting boundaries? Define your next steps for lasting transformation.

_____

_____

_____

_____

_____

_____

_____

_____

_____

_____

_____

_____

_____

_____

_____

_____

_____

_____

_____

_____

Daily Journal

Daily Journal

www.ingramcontent.com/pod-product-compliance
Lightning Source LLC
Chambersburg PA
CBHW041515120626

46551CB00018B/2443